WHAT CAN I DO WITH A MAJOR IN... **?**

How To *Choose* and *Use* Your College Major

- Careers graduates of the 21 most popular majors have entered from 1960 to the present

- Strategies for choosing your college major and planning your career

Lawrence R. Malnig, Ph.D.

Director/Counseling Center
SAINT PETER'S COLLEGE
With
Anita Malnig

With a Foreword by
Robert Hoppock, Ph.D.

Emeritus Professor
of Counselor Education
NEW YORK UNIVERSITY

Abbott Press   **Box 433**   **Ridgefield, N.J. 07657**

Printed and Published By

ABBOTT PRESS
P.O. BOX 433
RIDGEFIELD, N.J. 07657

Library of Congress Number: 83-73269

ISBN: Cloth: 0-9612678-1-X

ISBN: Paper: 0-9612678-0-1

Designed and Illustrated By Elizabeth Case
PRINTED IN THE UNITED STATES OF AMERICA

WHAT CAN I DO
WITH A MAJOR IN . . . ?

HOW TO *CHOOSE* AND *USE* YOUR COLLEGE MAJOR

ALL-NEW SELF-HELP FEATURES

✓   A personal self-assessment plan

✓   Selecting jobs that fit your personality

✓   Entry jobs for men/Entry jobs for women

✓   Avoiding the stereotyped major-to-job rut

✓   Expanding horizons — before and *after* college

*Get happiness out of your work or you may
never know what happiness is.*
                                    — Elbert Hubbard

To my family —
Laura, Anita, and Julie.

To my dear friend
— James A. Pegolotti —
who with care, compassion, and
respect for each one's individuality
helps students dare to be their best.

To the men and women graduates
of Saint Peter's College — whose
achievements made this book possible.

— ADEQUACY —

The spider spins his tapestries
With grey-blue threads of strength
And gives each silky filigree
Its necessary length.

So let me weave my sum of days
With fibers of strong thought
And give to every task of mine
The depth and breadth I ought.

ANTHONY NAVARRA

FOREWORD

A number of colleges have published follow-up reports on the jobs their seniors got after graduating. Some institutions have related this information to the respective college majors. These colleges deserve thanks and commendations from students, counselors, and parents for their institutional integrity in reporting what really happens to their product.

Malnig has gone much further. He has followed up alumni/alumnae for more than two decades, has reported entry-level jobs, and has then gone on to identify the career-jobs they subsequently moved into. In addition, the Holland Occupational Codes and Worker Functions Ratings he has associated with each job, in this completely new edition, will help readers expand their career prospects and identify the positions that are likely to match their personal needs and preferences. In doing that, he has provided a much-needed document that students, parents, and counselors all over the United States can use once again — this time even more specifically —to find out what a college graduate can do with his or her major in . . .

ROBERT HOPPOCK

ACKNOWLEDGMENTS

We thank the many colleagues and counselors across the country who so generously volunteered their suggestions for this new edition. We also appreciate the information we received from Robert Hoppock (New York University), John L. Holland (Johns Hopkins University), Jean Britton (University of Utah), Jo-Ida C. Hansen (University of Minnesota), Mildred Barker and Elaine Levy (New York State Department of Labor), Edward V. Collins, James J. Harrison, William A. Huebner, Eugene R. King, Martin H. Rosenbluth, Grace W. Schut and Richard D. Tetreau (Saint Peter's College), Marcia L. Mentkowski (Alverno College), Timothy Welles (Drew University), Bruce Riesenberg (University of California/Irvine), Henry Campbell (Jersey City State College), Robert Stump (Marymount College/Virginia), David H. Wilder (Bucknell University), Howard E. Mitchell (Wharton School, University of Pennsylvania), Heather Becker (University of Texas/Austin) and Robert Calvert (Garrett Park Press).

We also thank Eugene J. Kennedy, Lawrence R. Tormey, Michael M. Brown, Joan A. Malloy, and William K. Stoms, Jr. who helped in collecting our data; Gene N. Corbo and Barbara P. Mansfield for processing the results; and Peter M. Gotlieb for reviewing our manuscript. In the Counseling Center, our colleagues Lona Whitmarsh and Donald J. Marotto for their advice and moral support; Elizabeth Clossey, whose secretarial skills and constant good cheer make her a precious asset.

PREFACE

How people choose careers, prepare for them, and eventually prosper in them concerns most of us, directly or indirectly, throughout our lives. Helping students of all ages reach their goal of gainful employment involves those of us who teach, counsel, and train them, as well as those of us who foot the bill.

At one time or another, the list of individuals who find themselves caught up in career-planning includes, naturally enough, students in high school and college — both part-time and full-time. But it also takes into account, increasingly in our era, men and women planning to resume studies or even start college after years of life experience elsewhere.

Then there are career-changers, and those who are nearing retirement but want to go on putting their skills and insights to work in other fields of endeavor.

And professionally engaged in this intricate process of career-planning are high-school counselors and college counselors, placement officers, psychologists, social workers, clergy, psychiatrists, librarians, teachers and administrators at all educational levels, employment interviewers, campus recruiters, personnel managers, training and development officers, school trustees and legislators.

This list also includes those who have a personal interest in how career-planning turns out: husbands, wives, relatives, and parents.

This new, enlarged, and updated edition of "*What Can I Do With A Major In . . . ?*" brings together some of the most recent tools that career specialists, test-developers, and government agencies have devised to help people decide what they want to study and where they want to work.

In **Part One**, we explain the meaning of the numbers and letter-codes we use throughout this book to identify and classify jobs. Then we show how this ingenious system of numbers — taken from the United States Employment Service's *Dictionary of Occupational Titles* — and the letter codes, developed by John L. Holland to represent personality types, can help you relate your interests and personal preferences to satisfying, rewarding careers. We have also illustrated ways you can use these tools to help you make important educational decisions.

Part Two suggests how you can describe your interests and aptitudes in ways that enable you to identify those educational and career possibilities that may be open to *you* in particular. It also points out the pitfalls to avoid so you can make a positive, constructive evaluation of yourself.

Then in **Part Three**, we show how you can select from the later sections under each major — course descriptions, career leads, hiring institutions — whatever *you* may need to put *your* plans in focus.

In **Part Four**, each of the 21 majors we cover includes a list of the jobs that graduates of that major now hold, and separate columns for men and women showing the *beginning* jobs they got right after graduation.

And **Part Five** of *"What Can I Do With A Major In ... ?"* lists in alphabetical order, for easy reference, the jobs that graduates currently hold. Then it shows how many *different* majors each occupation draws on to fill its ranks.

In other words, we show you:

1. how to identify your personal skills and interests;

2. how to match your assets with jobs that require those assets;

3. the current trends in hiring people with your training; and,

4. how to put all this information to work for *you.*

While we suggest some ways to use our information and to assess your personal characteristics, we have not used up *all* the possibilities open to you by any means. You can put your imagination and ingenuity to work expanding those possibilities, without limit. You can begin, for example, by asking your best friends to predict your future career and to give you reasons for their choice — or you can experiment with your own combination of the number and letter codes we describe in Part One of this book.

We wish you well in this rewarding adventure. Like others, *you* too can make it — whatever your goal.

CONTENTS

v   FOREWORD BY ROBERT HOPPOCK

vi   ACKNOWLEDGMENTS

vii   PREFACE

1-4   INTRODUCTION

5 PART ONE

Meaning of Number and Letter Codes

27 PART TWO

Guide to Self-Assessment

37 PART THREE

How to Use:

    39   Description of Major

    41   Career Leads

    44   Hiring Institutions

    46   Current Occupations of Graduates

    47   Index: Major of Graduates by Occupation

51 PART FOUR

Careers by Departmental Major:

53 ACCOUNTANCY

59 ART HISTORY

63 BIOLOGY

71 CHEMISTRY

77 CLASSICS

81 ECONOMICS

91 EDUCATION

97 ENGLISH

105 HISTORY

113 MANAGEMENT

121 MARKETING

129 MATHEMATICS/COMPUTER SCIENCE

135 MODERN LANGUAGES

141 NATURAL SCIENCE

147 PHILOSOPHY

153 PHYSICS

159 POLITICAL SCIENCE

165 PSYCHOLOGY

171 SOCIOLOGY

177 URBAN STUDIES

183 PART FIVE

Index: Major of Graduates by Occupation

INTRODUCTION

T his book has been 15 years in the making. It began with an attempt to answer the most nagging question students at Saint Peter's College asked us:

- "What can I do with my major in . . . ?"

In our search for answers to this question, we raised some of our own:

- "Do graduates actually get the jobs we told them were available?"

- "What other jobs do they find?"

- "What are the more common beginning jobs?"

To get answers to these questions, we surveyed our alumni and, in 1968, we first reported the results in a mimeographed list showing the jobs that graduates of each major got. The results were quite unforeseen: Graduates were not landing the jobs one might reasonably expect. Yet the positive response we received from educators who said the well-worn copies of our report had captured considerable student interest, encouraged us to continue our research and to update our information. Seven years later we issued our first book-form edition of *"What Can I Do With A Major In . . . ?"* for national distribution.

In that 1975 Edition, we had occupations carry the numbers assigned to them in *The Dictionary of Occupational Titles* (DOT). We also had one listing, by major, for jobs alumni secured within five years after graduation, and another for occupations they held six to 25 years after leaving college.

We have expanded this current edition to include some of the suggestions counselors and other professional practitioners, nationwide, have sent us. Some liked particularly the research-based findings which confirm that liberal arts majors enter a wide variety of occupations; others said our factual data helped dispel stereotyped ideas about majors and careers. We have updated both categories of information in this, our 1984 Edition.

One of the helpful new touches in this Edition is a separate listing for the beginning jobs men and women got within five years after graduating. Another is the addition of DOT Worker Functions Ratings for each occupation. These ratings show the degree to which each job involves contact with *data, people,* and *things.*

We have also given each job a three-letter designation. This is the Holland Job Code which indicates the personality-type of people in that occupation. Holland uses the same code to describe the qualities of the work-environment because the surroundings reflect the personalities of the people who work there.

The meaning and uses of these classifications appear in the chapters that follow. But to put it briefly, by following the directions we have provided, readers can develop a personal letter-code that represents the kinds of activities and work environments they prefer. Then they can select careers listed under a major, or in the Index, which have the same letters as their personal three-letter code. The occupations the readers get by this matching process will identify those jobs that are likely to satisfy their needs.

The most surprising thing about our findings was the fact — which surfaced so consistently we couldn't help but be impressed by it — that regardless of their major, college graduates *enter a wide range of occupations, many of them seemingly unrelated to undergraduate studies.* These findings have forced us to conclude that *any* major, apparently, equips students with knowledge and skills that they can apply to a wide range of jobs in many diverse fields.

We have not been able to come up with easy explanations for this unexpected relationship between majors and careers. But that doesn't mean it's not important to develop accurate occupational information and to help students with careful academic planning. Quite the contrary. Besides information about the training and skill a job calls for, students need to know about the qualities that lead to success in a whole galaxy of occupations and how they can develop those qualities in a particular course of study, be it mathematics, psychology, or history. And they need to be aware of their personality traits and learn about the kinds of jobs that can accommodate those traits.

As we continued our research, we discovered that we were not alone in our findings about majors and careers. Colleges and universities across the country — CUNY, Mount Holyoke, Bucknell, Drew, Indiana, Utah, and California-Irvine — came up with similar results. This diversity of alumni jobs so impressed the authors of the Placement Office's Study at Indiana University that they titled their 1979 publication, *You Can Do Just About Anything.*

Another study now in progress seeks to discover which skills lead to career success and how one can incorporate them in college majors. This is taking place at Alverno College in Milwaukee, Wisconsin. Marcia L. Mentkowski and Austin Doherty issued an interim report on it in 1980 titled *Careering After College: Establishing the Validity of Abilities Learned in College for Later Success.* Their research aims to develop a competence model based on specific behaviors which make for success on a job. The investigators then plan to compare this model with the one they currently use at Alverno College and to suggest appropriate improvements.

The Wharton School of Finance at the University of Pennsylvania published in 1980 another pertinent study under the direction of Dr. Howard E. Mitchell, titled *The Extent and Nature of Vocational Change Among College Graduates: 1964-65 to 1977.* This investigation found that even technically-trained college graduates have many skills that transfer readily, and that the professional and technical skills we often associate with certain occupations are not so unique after all. The authors point out that "there appears to be a high degree of commonality of tasks as well as prerequisite skills between many seemingly different occupations which make transfers possible without major investments in formal education or training."

These studies support what we maintain here:

That students have a broad array of career opportunities open to them regardless of their major.

Nevertheless, planning a course of studies that will provide both immediately-marketable and long-range career skills is a difficult task for students today because of rising educational costs, uncertain economic conditions, and pressures from well-meaning parents and relatives to take "practical" courses. To accomplish this planning, besides examining all the objective data they have about careers, students also need to evaluate themselves:

- Do they like competitive or cooperative work situations?

- Are they happier working independently or in a structured environment?

- Do they prefer to speak and write, or to delve into facts and figures?

Our book offers several ways students can get this information and learn more about themselves, and then apply that information in choosing a compatible major, as well as in uncovering diverse career possibilities. A further bonus will be the discovery that, whichever major they've picked, the career possibilities under that major are surprisingly varied and virtually unlimited. Of course, this approach, as with any other, cannot guarantee job success. But as a method based on accurate information about jobs and ways to increase self-awareness, it will enable readers to move ahead with greater confidence and a heightened sense of direction.

We hope our research will serve as a useful guide for both students and the counselors who always look for better ways to help them. We wish those students fulfillment and success in the choices they make. We know from experience that counselors will get *their* fulfillment from seeing how they had a hand in helping their students achieve their goals.

L.R.M.

PART ONE
MEANING OF NUMBER AND LETTER CODES

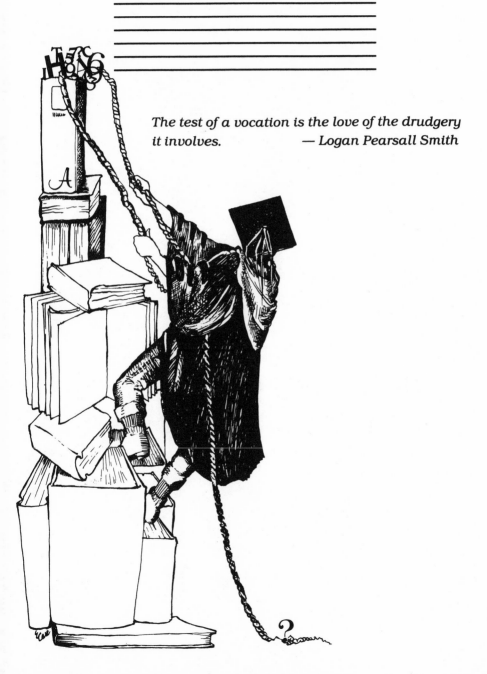

The test of a vocation is the love of the drudgery it involves.
— *Logan Pearsall Smith*

PART ONE
MEANING OF NUMBER
AND LETTER CODES

E ach of the occupations you will find listed in this book has the same six-digit number as the one the United States Government Publication *The Dictionary of Occupational Titles* (DOT) assigns to it. The Dictionary's Fourth and current Edition (1977) contains extensive definitions of some 20,000 jobs. This numerical classification system gives each occupation its own separate and distinct number. This arrangement makes it possible for the reader to get a complete picture of any occupation we mention in this book by looking up the number the DOT assigns to that job.

Each occupation we have listed has two sets of three-digit numbers separated by a decimal — for example, Accountant *160.167*. The first three numbers classify the job. The second three indicate how much it involves contact with *data, people,* and *things*. We'll have more to say about that later.

Besides these numbers, each occupation has a three-*letter* code. This code is from a classification system which John L. Holland, the noted vocational psychologist, originated.

Holland's letters follow the DOT's numerical designation like this: Accountant 160.167 *CES*. His letters indicate, in descending order, the more pronounced characteristics of both the people who hold those jobs and the environment where they do the work. Take the Accountant's letters, for example: The "C" stands for Conventional (orderly), which is the most common trait of people in this occupation. The work environment also reflects this orderliness. Next comes "E" for Enterprising — a prevalent but less common trait in accountants. And "S" for Social, a quality fewer accountants possess compared to the first two. The letters do not mean you will need these traits to be an accountant. They show only which of the six traits in this classification system accountants are most likely to have.

Below you will find other examples. We also explain in more detail the numbering system itself, and the meaning of the six letters which make up Holland's Summary Occupational Code.

Numerical Classification

The three digits in front of the decimal classify 1) the job's broad *category*, 2) its *subdivisions*, and 3) the specific *group* the job belongs to. For example, the number for Food Chemist is 022. The first digit, ZERO, tells you it comes under the heading of Professional, Technical, and Managerial positions. The second digit, TWO, narrows it down to occupations in Mathematics and the Physical Sciences. And the third number, also a TWO in this case, tells us that this occupation is in the more precise subgroup of Jobs in Chemistry.

In *The Dictionary Of Occupational Titles*, nine broad first-digit categories classify most occupations. These categories are:

0 and 1. Professional, Technical, Managerial

2. Clerical and Sales

3. Service

4. Agricultural, Fishery, Forestry, and Related

5. Processing

6. Machine Trades

7. Benchwork

8. Structural Work

9. Miscellaneous

These nine categories break down into 82 subdivisions by adding a second digit. Take the number 07. The first number 0 indicates a Professional, Technical or Managerial occupation, and the second number 7 shows it's in the subdivision of Medicine and Health. Then, by adding a third digit, you can expand these 82 subdivisions into 559 smaller, homogeneous groups. In the number 075, for instance, the five would further indicate that *Registered Nurses* constitute a subgroup of occupations in Medicine and Health.

Since only college graduates hold the jobs we list in this book, you can expect that most of those jobs will fall under the first category of Professional, Technical and Managerial occupations. When this category splits up into the narrower subdivisions we have illustrated above, the number of the different occupational groups under this heading expands to 100. We have listed those 100 three-digit subgroups below.

We have also listed the 60 three-digit subgroups that appear under Clerical and Sales Occupations, because it is in this area that many college graduates have found both beginning jobs and, eventually, careers such as Computer Operations Supervisor (213), Insurance Claims Adjuster (241) and Pharmaceutical Detailer (262), to name just a few.

THREE-DIGIT OCCUPATIONAL GROUPS
The Dictionary of Occupational Titles p. xxxvi

PROFESSIONAL, TECHNICAL, AND MANAGERIAL OCCUPATIONS

00/01
Occupations in architecture, engineering, and surveying

001 Architectural occupations

002 Aeronautical engineering occupations

003 Electrical/electronics engineering occupations

005 Civil engineering occupations

006 Ceramic engineering occupations

007 Mechanical engineering occupations

008 Chemical engineering occupations

010 Mining and petroleum engineering occupations

011 Metallurgy and metallurgical occupations

012 Industrial engineering occupations

013 Agricultural engineering occupations

014 Marine engineering occupations

015 Nuclear engineering occupations

017 Drafters, n.e.c.*

018 Surveying/cartographic occupations

*Not elsewhere classified

019 Occupations in architecture, engineering, and surveying, n.e.c.

02
Occupations in mathematics and physical sciences

020 Occupations in mathematics

021 Occupations in astronomy

022 Occupations in chemistry

023 Occupations in physics

024 Occupations in geology

025 Occupations in meteorology

029 Occupations in mathematics and physical sciences, n.e.c.

04
Occupations in life sciences

040 Occupations in agricultural sciences

041 Occupations in biological sciences

045 Occupations in psychology

049 Occupations in life sciences, n.e.c.

05
Occupations in social sciences

050 Occupations in economics

051 Occupations in political science

052 Occupations in history

054 Occupations in sociology

055 Occupations in anthropology

059 Occupations in social sciences, n.e.c.

07
Occupations in medicine and health

070 Physicians and surgeons

071 Osteopaths

072 Dentists

073 Veterinarians

074 Pharmacists

075 Registered nurses

076 Therapists

077 Dietitians

078 Occupations in medical and dental technology

079 Occupations in medicine and health, n.e.c.

09
Occupations in education

090 Occupations in college and university education

091 Occupations in secondary school education

092 Occupations in preschool, primary school, and kindergarten education

094 Occupations in education of the handicapped

096 Home economists and farm advisers

097 Occupations in vocational education, n.e.c.

099 Occupations in education, n.e.c.

10
Occupations in museum, library, and archival sciences

100 Librarians

101 Archivists

102 Museum curators and related occupations

109 Occupations in museum, library, and archival sciences, n.e.c.

11
Occupations in law and jurisprudence

110 Lawyers

111 Judges

119 Occupations in law and jurisprudence, n.e.c.

12
Occupations in religion and theology

120 Clergy

129 Occupations in religion and theology, n.e.c.

13
Occupations in writing

131 Writers

132 Editors: publication, broadcast, and script

137 Interpreters and translators

139 Occupations in writing, n.e.c.

14
Occupations in art

141 Commercial artists: designers and illustrators, graphic arts

142 Environmental, product, and related designers

143 Occupations in photography

144 Fine artists: painters, sculptors, and related occupations

149 Occupations in art, n.e.c.

15
Occupations in entertainment and recreation

150 Occupations in dramatics

151 Occupations in dancing

152 Occupations in music

153 Occupations in athletics and sports

159 Occupations in entertainment and recreation, n.e.c.

16
Occupations in administrative specializations

160 Accountants and auditors

161 Budget and management systems analysis occupations

162 Purchasing management occupations

163 Sales and distribution management occupations

164 Advertising management occupations

165 Public relations management occupations

166 Personnel administration occupations

168 Inspectors and investigators, managerial and public service

169 Occupations in administrative specializations, n.e.c.

18
Managers and officials, n.e.c.

180 Agriculture, forestry, and fishing industry managers and officials

181 Mining industry managers and officials

182 Construction industry managers and officials

183 Manufacturing industry managers and officials

184 Transportation, communication, and utilities industry managers and officials

185 Wholesale and retail trade managers and officials

186 Finance, insurance, and real estate managers and officials

187 Service industry managers and officials

188 Public administration managers and officials

189 Miscellaneous managers and officials, n.e.c.

19
Miscellaneous professional, technical, and managerial occupations

191 Agents and appraisers, n.e.c.

193 Radio operators

194 Sound, film, and videotape recording, and reproduction occupations

195 Occupations in social and welfare work

196 Airplane pilots and navigators

197 Ship captains, mates, pilots and engineers

198 Railroad conductors

199 Miscellaneous professional, technical, and managerial occupations, n.e.c.

CLERICAL AND SALES OCCUPATIONS

20
Stenography, typing, filing and related occupations

201 Secretaries

202 Stenographers

203 Typists and typewriting-machine operators

205 Interviewing clerks

206 File clerks

207 Duplicating-machine operators and tenders

208 Mailing and miscellaneous office machine operators

209 Stenography, typing, filing, and related occupations

21
Computing and account-recording occupations

210 Bookkeepers and bookkeeping-machine operators

211 Cashiers and tellers

213 Electronic and electro-mechanical data processors

214 Billing and rate clerks

215 Payroll, timekeeping, and duty-roster clerks

216 Accounting and statistical clerks

217 Account-recording-machine operators, n.e.c.

219 Computing and account-recording occupations, n.e.c.

22
Production and stock clerks and related occupations

221 Production clerks

222 Shipping, receiving, stock, and related clerical occupations

229 Production and stock clerks and related occupations, n.e.c.

23
Information and message distribution occupations

230 Hand delivery and distribution occupations

235 Telephone operators

236 Telegraph operators

237 Information and reception clerks

238 Accommodation clerks and gate and ticket agents

239 Information and message distribution occupations, n.e.c.

24
Miscellaneous clerical occupations

241 Investigators, adjusters, and related occupations

243 Government service clerks, n.e.c.

245 Medical service clerks, n.e.c.

247 Advertising-service clerks, n.e.c.

248 Transportation-service clerks, n.e.c.

249 Miscellaneous clerical occupations, n.e.c.

25
Sales occupations, services

250 Sales occupations, real estate and insurance

251 Sales occupations, business and financial services

252 Sales occupations, transportation services

253 Sales occupations, utilities

254 Sales occupations, printing and advertising

259 Sales occupations, services, n.e.c.

26
Sales occupations, consumable commodities

260 Sales occupations, agricultural and food products

261 Sales occupations, textile products, apparel, and notions

262 Sales occupations, chemicals, drugs, and sundries

269 Sales occupations, miscellaneous consumable commodities, n.e.c.

27
Sales occupations, commodities, n.e.c.

270 Sales occupations, home furniture, furnishings, and appliances

271 Sales occupations, electrical goods, except home appliances

272 Sales occupations, farm and gardening equipment and supplies

273 Sales occupations, transportation equipment, parts, and supplies

274 Sales occupations, industrial and related equipment and supplies

275 Sales occupations, business and commercial equipment and supplies

276 Sales occupations, medical and scientific equipment and supplies

277 Sales occupations, sporting, hobby, stationery, and related goods

279 Sales occupations, miscellaneous commodities, n.e.c.

29
Miscellaneous sales occupations

290 Sales clerks

291 Vending and door to door selling occupations

292 Route sales and delivery occupations

293 Solicitors

294 Auctioneers

295 Rental clerks

296 Shoppers

297 Sales promotion occupations

298 Merchandise displayers

299 Miscellaneous sales occupations, n.e.c.

We have not listed the subdivisions of the other seven categories because not many college graduates find jobs in them. Those who do establish careers in the service occupations, for instance, go in mostly for the Protective Services, 373-376, such as Firefighter, Special Agent, etc. Those in the remaining categories usually enter the Skilled Trades.

An important thing to keep in mind is that the 100 listings under Professional, Technical and Managerial occupations refer to *groups* of occupations rather than to the *number* of individual jobs. For example, the group 024, Occupations in Geology, contains all the individual occupations that have something to do with the earth's crust. It includes jobs such as Hydrologist, Mineralogist, Seismologist, and even Prospector — 17 in all. But the number of jobs for each group varies. The 070 group, Physicians and Surgeons, contains 26 specific jobs while 055, Anthropology, has only five. When we add all the individual jobs these 100 groups list, we get a total of some 1,500 separate titles for the Professional, Technical, and Managerial category.

When numerous occupations have the same three-digit designation, the DOT lists them according to how much the job involves contact with *data, people,* and *things.* The second set of three digits indicates that, and we explain how it does so in the next section.

For example, under the three-digit group 160, the DOT lists 17 different jobs for Accountants and Auditors. The one at the head of the list, Tax Accountant 160.*162,* involves the most direct contact with *data, people,* and *things,* while the one at the bottom — Estimator 160.*267* — involves the least.

Worker Functions Ratings

The second set of three digits, separated from the first set by a decimal, indicates, as we have said, how much someone in that job has to deal with *data, people,* and *things.*

The first number after the decimal refers to *data,* the second to *people,* and the third to *things.* These numbers range from 0 to 8. The lower numbers indicate the more complex functions —those that call for a higher degree of responsibility and judgment.

For instance, under Data, Analyzing bears a TWO. But Copying is a less complicated function, so it bears a FIVE.

Here are the three categories, together with the specific functions the DOT lists for them in descending order of complexity:

Data	People	Things
0 Synthesizing	0 Mentoring	0 Setting Up
1 Coordinating	1 Negotiating	1 Precision Work
2 Analyzing	2 Instructing	2 Operating, Controlling
3 Compiling	3 Supervising	3 Driving/Operating
4 Computing	4 Diverting	4 Manipulating
5 Copying	5 Persuading	5 Tending
6 Comparing	6 Speaking/ Signaling	6 Feeding/Offbearing
	7 Serving	7 Handling
	8 Taking Instruction/Helping	

DATA

The first category, *Data*, refers to all types of information: words, numbers, ideas, concepts — known or assumed — from which one draws conclusions. Each of the six terms under this category tells the way one can work with data or information. Here are the definitions and some illustrations of those terms:

0 Synthesizing: Understanding, utilizing, and assimilating data to uncover, discover, perform certain tasks, and develop and create new ideas, concepts, etc.

Example: A *Safety Engineer* — 010.061 — for mines and quarries synthesizes vital information. He must inspect mines, and if he finds that anything is not up to safety standards, he must use principles of mining-engineering to correct the situation.

1 Coordinating: Determining time, place, and sequence of operations or action to be taken on the basis of analysis of data; executing that determination and/or reporting on events.

> Example: A *Radio, TV, or Movie Producer* — 159.117 — coordinates data. This person selects script-writers, equipment, and staff to take care of costumes, props, music. The producer reviews scripts and coordinates sound, script, photography, and other elements of production.

2 Analyzing: Examining and evaluating data. Presenting alternative actions in relation to the evaluation.

> Example: A *Police Officer* — 375.263 — especially on patrol, must size up an accident or a crime in progress and take appropriate steps.

3 Compiling: Gathering, collating, or classifying information. Reporting and/or carrying out a prescribed action in relation to that information.

> Example: A *Teller* — 211.362 — receives and pays out money, verifies amounts, and examines checks for endorsements. Keeps records of money, computes service charges, and issues receipts.

Here are the definitions of the remaining functions in this category:

4 Computing: Performing arithmetic operations and reporting on and/or carrying out a prescribed action in relation to them.

5 Copying: Transcribing, entering, or posting data.

6 Comparing: Examining the characteristics of data, people, or things to find out how they differ and what they have in common.

PEOPLE

This second category, *People*, describes the type of roles involved in working with people. It also includes dealing with animals on an individual basis as if they were humans, i.e., the way veterinarians do.

0 Mentoring: Giving advice and counsel to people for problems that may require legal, scientific, clinical, spiritual, or professional principles for their solution.

> Example: A *Criminal Lawyer* — 110.107 — deals with offenses against the state or society (theft, murder, arson). Such a lawyer interviews clients and witnesses to ascertain facts, prosecutes or defends the accused against charges, summarizes case to jury.

1 Negotiating: Exchanging ideas and information with others to formulate policies and jointly to arrive at decisions, conclusions, solutions.

> Example: The *Head Coach* of an athletic team — 153.117 —must evaluate players' skills and assign team positions accordingly; the coach also helps decide on trades and recruiting.

2 Instructing: Teaching, informing, educating by showing, lecturing, or guiding someone's performance.

> Example: A *Home Economist* — 096.121 —advises consumers, community groups, or homemakers on matters of nutrition, clothing, and other household concerns. This person may teach in schools, do research, or write instructive articles.

3 Supervising: Being in charge of a staff, assigning specific duties to them, maintaining harmonious relations among them, and promoting efficiency.

> Example: A *Recreation Supervisor* — 187.137 — coordinates and takes charge of many

types of recreational facilities. This person develops the recreational programs, hires personnel for activities, and oversees the entire process.

The definitions of the other functions in this category are as follows:

4 Diverting: Amusing others, usually on stage, television, in movies, on radio.

5 Persuading: Influencing others in favor of a product, service, or point of view.

6 Speaking/Signaling: Talking to people to give or receive information; also giving assignments or directions to helpers and assistants.

7 Serving: Taking care of the needs of people or animals, usually with immediate response.

8 Taking Instruction/Helping: Acting directly on instructions from a supervisor, with no responsibility involved.

THINGS

The last category, *Things*, lists the ways people can interact with inanimate objects in a work situation. Inanimate objects include tools, machines, equipment, and goods.

0 Setting Up: Altering and fixing equipment so that it is ready to do the job it was designed to do.

Example: A *Photo-Optics Technician* — 029.280 — sets and uses photo-optical equipment to photograph data for scientists and engineers. This involves doing detailed work according to specific diagrams and already-established procedures.

1 Precision Working: Manually using tools and/or equipment to bring about a specific end, and using skill and judgement in building the tools and equipment.

Example: A *Stained Glass Artist* — 142.061 — prepares and cuts glass to render a particular picture or design. The work involves cutting, waxing, painting, firing, and sometimes installing the finished window.

2 Operating and Controlling: Starting, stopping, and controlling the movement of machines or equipment. The operator of the equipment also sets up the machines and controls temperature, speed, pressure, etc.

Example: A *Telegrapher* — 236.562 — works the telegraph key and teletype machines to give and receive train orders, and keeps track of time, dates, and locations.

3 Driving/Operating: Steering and guiding the movement of equipment that fabricates things or moves people. The operator must watch dials and gauges, and judge distances.

Example: An *Airplane Pilot* — 196.263 — directs changes in fuel, load, and route; reads dials; makes sure all equipment is operating to assure maximum safety; runs through pre-flight checklist, etc.

And here are the definitions of all the other functions under this category.

4 Manipulating: Using one's body or tools to move, guide, or locate objects. Involves some judgment, but someone else usually lays out the work.

5 Tending: Starting, stopping, and adjusting controls of machines — e.g., flipping switches, turning dials — without having to exercise critical judgment in making those adjustments.

6 Feeding/Offbearing: Placing, throwing, or putting objects or materials into equipment which other operators run or which is automatic.

7 Handling: Handling involves only small contact with things. One might use one's body or simple tools to move or carry objects.

Let us return to the Food Chemist (022.061) for one last specific example of Worker Functions Ratings. In the full number following the decimal, the ZERO tells us that someone in this position *synthesizes* data; the second number, SIX, indicates a relatively minimal interaction with people, *speaking and signaling*; and the last number, ONE, shows that the job involves exercising considerable judgment and responsibility in dealing with things — *operating and controlling.*

What's especially interesting about the Worker Functions Ratings is that a particular pattern can be present in a variety of different occupations, as well as within related ones. Consequently, it's helpful in exploring occupations to have an idea of how much and in what capacity you would like to work with *data, people,* and *things.* It can be quite enlightening to see how the same second set of digits can accompany very different occupations. For instance, while the first three digits for Camp Director, 195, and Credit Manager, 168, are quite different, the second set of digits, 167, is the same for each. This means that while Credit Manager is mainly a business occupation and a Camp Director works in a social environment, both occupations involve the same degree of contact with *data, people,* and *things.* This kind of knowledge may open up new occupational possibilities for the reader to consider.

OCCUPATIONAL CODES

In addition to the six DOT numbers, each occupation in this book has a three-letter designation. These letters, as we have mentioned, indicate the personality characteristics most typical of people in that occupation, as well as the dominant features of the environment in which these people do their work. Personality and work environments resemble one another, according to Holland's theory, because people seek out work surroundings that please them. And once in the job, workers tend to modify that environment in ways that reflect their personalities.

For instance, a person scoring high on the social scale may derive satisfaction from helping others, as would a Licensed Practical Nurse. While taking care of others, this same person will help to create caring, nurturing conditions within the work situation.

John L. Holland, the vocational psychologist who originated this theory, reasoned that people in our culture could be classified under six broad categories which he labeled Realistic, Investigative, Artistic, Social, Enterprising, and Conventional (RIASEC). Each person, according to this theory, can be classified by a combination of these six types. For practical purposes, however, only the three letters representing the most pronounced traits are used to classify an occupation. For instance, a motion picture director would have the letter code AES: Artistic first of all, Enterprising next, and Social third.

The traits represented by these six types often develop from a person's long-term interests and experiences. For example, someone who as a child had chemistry sets, did scientific experiments, and won prizes at science fairs might very well carry over that interest into adult life. Holland would theorize that this person who had a strong scientific leaning —which Holland labels investigative — would probably function well in a work environment requiring this trait.

No one person possesses *only* the characteristics of one type, any more than we can say there are *only* six distinct types of people. People are complex, naturally enough, and display interesting combinations of these traits. Moreover, these personality definitions, described below, represent the *extreme* tendencies of a type, in order to emphasize how each personality description is different from the next.

But, these six categories can help you think constructively about your own tendencies: The classifications may help sharpen your focus on specific traits you possess and lead you to ways to use them best. For instance, you may become aware that your high rating on the social scale, based on your knack of making friends easily, is an ability you can use well in teaching or sales occupations.

Here is a listing of the six categories, with some of the

personal qualities related to each, and examples of the occupations that include people with these traits.

Realistic:

Realistic people prefer physical work and therefore are often physically strong and rugged. They also enjoy working with their hands, using tools and machines; frequently enough, this work takes them outdoors. Some occupations in which you'll find this type of person are: mechanical and construction jobs, technical laboratory jobs, agricultural/wildlife occupations, police work, skilled trades.

Here are some adjectives describing realistic people: stable, frank, genuine, practical, persistent, thrifty, natural. Some specific examples:

> **Ship Pilot** — 197.133, *REI* — Realistic first, Enterprising next, Investigative third.

> **Firefighter** — 373.364, *RSE* — Realistic first, Social second, Enterprising last.

Investigative:

The investigative person likes to observe, analyze, and solve problems, particularly in scientific and mathematical areas. This person probably is a creative thinker who would enjoy working with ideas, words and symbols, and might also like doing this work alone.

Some occupations in which you'd find this type of person are: psychologist, biologist, meteorologist, chemist.

Here are some descriptive adjectives associated with this theme: analytical, curious, independent, intellectual, precise, rational. Some specific examples:

> **Pharmacist** — 074.161, *IES* — Investigative first, Enterprising second, Social last.

> **Computer Programer** — 020.187, *IAS* — Investigative first, Artistic second, Social third.

Artistic:

The artistic person is likely to be unconventional and original in outlook and does self-expressive, creative work in any of the arts. Use of imagination is important to these people.

Artistic professions include artist, author, singer, dancer, poet, and music conductor.

Some of the adjectives describing artistic people are: expressive, imaginative, intuitive, introspective, original, non-conforming. And some specific examples are:

> **Music Conductor** — 152.047, *ASI* — Artistic first, Social second, Investigative last.

> **Dancing Teacher** — 151.027, *ASE* — Artistic first, Social second, Enterprising third.

Social:

Social people enjoy working with other people and are generally responsible, popular, and concerned about the well-being of others. These people also like to inform, train, and cure, and handle problems by talking about and examining relationships and feelings.

Social occupations include family counselors, sociologists, parole officers, camp directors.

Some of the adjectives associated with this theme are: cooperative, friendly, generous, helpful, idealistic, insightful, kind, and understanding. Some specific occupations are:

> **Clergy member** — 120.007, *SAI* — Social first, Artistic second, Investigative last.

> **Bartender** — 312.474, *SEC* — Social first, Enterprising next, Conventional third.

Enterprising:

The enterprising person, like the social person, also enjoys working with people. In this capacity, however, it is to influence, to persuade, to manage — and very often for economic gain. Such people are energetic and adventurous and often like material success, power, and status.

Enterprising occupations include stockbroker, television producer, salesperson, politician.

Some adjectives describing these people are: adventurous, ambitious, energetic, optimistic, self-confident, sociable, talkative. Specific examples are:

> **Commissary Manager** — 185.167, *ESI* — Enterprising first, Social second, Investigative last.

> **Building Contractor** — 182.167 *ERI* — Enterprising first, Realistic next, Investigative third.

Conventional:

Conventional people like working with data and often have good clerical and mechanical skills. They tend to work well in large organizations, following through on others' instructions and carrying out details.

Conventional professions include: auditor, proofreader, bank teller, statistician, bursar.

Adjectives describing conventional people are: conscientious, careful, orderly, persistent, practical, calm. Specific examples are:

> **Budget Accountant** — 160.167, *CES* — Conventional first, Enterprising second, Social last.

> **Secretary** — 201.362, *CSA* — Conventional first, Social second, Artistic last.

These numbers and letter codes can help you narrow down the work areas that attract you most and which you may want to examine more carefully.

The worker-functions ratings will enable you to identify those jobs within your area of interest which involve the degree of contact with *data, people,* and *things* you would find agreeable.

In addition, by examining the descriptions of the letter codes you can decide on the two or three which most closely describe you as you see yourself. Then, by putting these letters in order of rank to get your personal theme or code, you can see how closely it matches the code of the occupations you had selected on the basis of the DOT numbers.

In the next section, on self-assessment, you will find some more detailed guidelines for career exploration, as well as information about tests and counseling services that can assist you.

PART TWO

GUIDE TO
SELF-ASSESSMENT

Millionaires are successful because they do what they like and they do it well. — Malcolm Forbes

PART TWO
GUIDE TO SELF-ASSESSMENT

N ow that you have an idea of how the mechanics of this book work, you'll want to go on and get a better idea about yourself and how you can use this information to your advantage in planning a career. Just where do you begin this search for career fulfillment?

The best place to start is with **yourself**.

Begin your career search by taking a long, accurate — and positive — look at yourself. Your quest is to discover interests and abilities which will be your tools for carving out your career. But self-assessment, like any other kind of self-confrontation, is easier said than done.

"Why does it seem so difficult to figure out what I'm interested in?" you might ask.

Why? Because we've often found that people struggle to measure up to unreasonable expectations they've set for themselves or that others have set for them, usually without realizing it. Some people get nervous at the thought of listing their skills and strong points. "Do I really have any?"

Others avoid any kind of self-examination because they fear they'll find out for sure that they indeed have all the shortcomings they suspect they do.

Still others hesitate to look at themselves because, unlike the self-doubters, they don't want to believe they have even a single flaw. The slightest imperfection, they feel, would make them worthless!

Both types of person hold back from this self-examination, often without knowing the underlying reason why.

Even if you don't fall directly into one of these more extreme groups, this kind of thinking may keep you from taking that important first step: accepting yourself as you are.

Once you allow yourself to become tolerant and realistic about yourself, you'll find self-assessment to be an interesting process, full of surprises. If you accept your strengths and your weaknesses, your assets *as well as* your liabilities, you'll begin to move.

Dwelling on faults and failures can only make you over-look the *positive* qualities you've developed. Whether you're an 18-year-old freshman trying to select a major, a 35-year-old homemaker trying to get up the nerve to enroll in college, or someone considering retirement, the human tendency to play down one's assets haunts each one of us.

When we ask students how they feel about the person they see in the mirror each day, we often hear a long list of faults. But when we ask them about their good qualities, they lose their tongues. Then they look puzzled and surprised when we tell them their records show they persevered long enough to complete elementary and high school, their performance sur-passed that of half the students in their graduating class, they made friends easily, and they had notable talents in verbal and linguistic subjects. All these positive pieces of information just from a transcript!

Homemakers over 30 or 35, away from school for a long time, also have trouble identifying their assets. They do not always see how their achievements in the home and community sprang from talents they can now further develop by coming back to school. They don't always understand that their ability to organize and schedule family activities, for instance, or to carry out a successful fund-raising campaign for the local church, or to teach arts and crafts to club members add up to aptitudes and abilities they can use in furthering their college studies. For instance, if you're the one who takes care of the family's finances, you might want to extend that talent to the study of accounting or economics. The old song "Accentuate the Positive" still holds true. Emphasizing the negative only short-circuits your awareness of qualities that can help you look ahead with purpose and self-confidence.

Even so, it's not so easy to dismiss negative myths about oneself. When we point out a skill in solving computa-tional problems or learning a new language, for instance, stu-dents will say it doesn't count because they did not have to try very hard. In other words, if you don't struggle over something it can't be worthwhile. They do not see that the task that comes easily to them may be difficult for someone else, and that their ability to do it with ease shows they have an aptitude they can build on.

This self-belittling behavior should not come as a surprise in the face of child-rearing and educational practices of parents and teachers that still devote more attention to detecting faults than to discovering and developing one's unique gifts and talents. Drawing attention to what someone has done well — what psychologists call positive reinforcement — is not a common practice, unfortunately, either in the classroom or on the job.

Another reason for this tendency we all have to be excessively self-critical is that we have let ourselves become conditioned to trying to measure up to what others expect of us. That way, without realizing it, we make other people's goals our own. For instance, we might believe we have to be the kind of doctor or lawyer our parents talk about so glowingly, or that we must at least match the income of cousin Phil or Rachel, or live in a fancy neighborhood with a Mercedes-Benz in the driveway. Under such pressures, it becomes impossible to define our own values, so we become unable to recognize, let alone question, the demands we unwittingly impose on ourselves. And, if we fail to live up to these unquestioned and unarticulated expectations, we begin to develop feelings of depression and futility, but with no idea where they are coming from.

So, it's vitally important to take stock, to get to know your likings and limitations, and to accept a realistic evaluation of yourself. Once you get beyond this web of negativity, of unreal expectations and exaggerated deficits, and begin to add up your true assets and interests, you will begin to experience a dramatic change in your attitude about yourself.

How to discover those assets and interests? Here's one way to begin your personal audit: List everything you did the day before — at home, at work, at play, at school. You eased an unyielding door. Did you really enjoy it? You shopped for a coat, read the paper, paid the bills, translated your French assignment and sketched your teacher's face in your notebook. How did you enjoy each activity? How did you feel when each was finished? Which ones did you do particularly well? Keep your list going. These activities can be physical, social, intellectual. They can involve speaking, writing, using your hands, thinking, or just imaginative daydreaming. These lists will start you thinking of yourself in a positive way as you focus on your accomplishments and capabilities.

Once you put your mind to it, you will find many other ways to tune in on your interests. For example, when you read a daily paper or a newsmagazine, which section do you go to first? And in what order do you read the other sections? Do you scour the Financial Section first, pick through the Book Reviews, and then skim over national and international news? Or do you spend most of your reading time absorbing new discoveries in science and technology, and devote what time remains to working out quizzes and puzzles?

Note, also, how deeply you plunge into any subject you like. Which ones do you talk about to your friends or go to the library to look up in greater detail? Do you actively seek out people who share your liking for, say, opera, politics, or space exploration? These are all good indicators of the nature and strength of your interests.

In your search, it is also important to pay attention to those areas of human endeavor you generally tend to ignore. This is a case where your negatives can have positive value for you. If you notice, for instance, that you would never know the difference if the Business or Travel Sections of your Sunday *Times* were missing, you can be sure that these subjects do not hold much educational or career interest for you. In other words, *it is equally useful to be aware of what you dislike* intensely and do poorly. This kind of information can save you the time you would waste following fruitless leads.

At this point, you might want to refer back to the description of number and letter codes. Suppose you've discovered that you spend some of your most enjoyable time with people —working in clubs, organizing groups, even giving parties. Review in detail the People Section under Worker Functions

Ratings to get an idea of all the ways you can interact with people in a work situation.

Then, in the section on the Holland Letter Codes, read about the Social Theme. How do these descriptions fit in with your own personality assessment? Are you getting a clearer picture of yourself?

If you follow the suggestions we have made, at this point you should have a rather detailed summary of your current preferences and leanings as they relate to most academic and vocational areas.

Now the question is — how do you go about linking this knowledge to a suitable course of study or the choice of a future career? How can you know if your attraction to mathematics, or writing, for example, will continue, or if you have the ability to succeed in either of these fields of study?

Don't fret. Just keep ferreting out everything you know about yourself. Look at your past history: school activities, summer jobs, leisure-time pursuits, hobbies and community activities. Which kind of tasks held your interest consistently over a long period of time? What skills did you use most, and which ones were superior compared to those of people around you?

In school, for example, which homework assignments did you like to do first? And in what subjects did answers come to you quickly? While you may not have paid particular attention to it at the time, you probably were aware that in classes you looked forward to attending because you did so well, there were some students who dreaded being there and had to struggle to get passing grades. These are the indicators that will point out your most prominent skills and interests, the ones that have endured. They are the best predictors of what you will *continue* to like and do well.

Whether your skills are verbal or computational, you are not likely to lose them later on, nor are they likely to atrophy because you have been away from school for a long period of time. What you've done now has been to catalog your current interests and find out if you have the drive and the abilities you will need to sustain those interests.

Strengthened by this knowledge, you can now tackle the task of finding suitable educational and career objectives with greater assurance and a firmer sense of direction.

Whether you are in school, at home, or holding down a job in business, there is another route you can follow in doing your career audit. You can take a "test" or interest inventory, either by yourself or with the assistance of a counselor. Simply contact the high school, college, United States Employment Service or community agency nearest you to get the help you need.

One interest inventory you can score and evaluate yourself is the Self-Directed Search (SDS) by John L. Holland, the vocational psychologist whose Occupational Letter code we've described for you. The advantage of this inventory is that it enables you to do your own scoring, profiling, and interpretation so you can get immediate results. Holland also has a companion booklet titled *The Occupations Finder* which lists occupations according to their letter codes.

If you've worked out your personality letter-code, you can see what occupations are listed under that code in *The Occupations Finder.* In addition, each of the 500 occupations that Holland lists in his booklet under the different combinations of three-letter codes is accompanied by the six-digit code it carries in the DOT. This makes it possible for you to go to *The Dictionary of Occupational Titles* to look up additional jobs under the DOT numbers that appear most frequently under your letter code.

The Strong-Campbell Interest Inventory (SCII) is another "test" you can take to help you in your career search. This Inventory calls for the services of a professional counselor to interpret the results, which require machine scoring.

The results of your Interest Inventory appear in a profile which has 162 occupational scales arranged under the six general occupational themes based on Holland's personality types. From this profile, you can obtain your own occupational letter-code as well as an indication of how closely your career interests resemble those of people who like the job they hold.

Since this profile has separate norms for men and

women, in most jobs you can compare your scores with those of members of your own sex. Each of these aids can increase your prospects of finding a satisfying course of study or a career.

If you use both these inventories you will note that in some instances the SDS and the SCII assign different letter codes to the same occupation. Holland explains that these letter codes can be useful but that they are *changeable* approximations that will constantly undergo revision as research continues. When discrepancies do occur, Holland advises that you read the job and code descriptions and then use your own judgment in arriving at a letter code for the occupation.

There are also other interest inventories available to you through the agencies we have mentioned. These two inventories, however, are the most popular and rest on solid research that has been going on for many years. But bear in mind that no test or inventory can perform magic. Carefully think things through for yourself first. That way, inventories can give you good leads to explore your future career possibilities.

PART THREE

HOW TO USE —
- Description of Major
- Career Leads
- Hiring Institutions
- Current Occupations of Graduates
- Major of Graduates by Occupation

A new principle is an inexhaustible source of new views. — *Vauvenargues*

PART THREE
DESCRIPTION OF MAJOR

S tudents often have the wrong idea about the meaning and subject matter of the curriculum in which they plan to major. Time after time, students change majors or drop out of school because they did not foresee that accounting, for example, would require more than basic numerical computations, that physics would have so much mathematics, or that nursing brings you so much into contact with sick people.

To help you avoid making such mistakes, we have provided a short, clear definition of each discipline or major. These definitions identify the key characteristics of a major that distinguish it from all the others. We have emphasized *differences* rather than similarities to help you avoid confusion.

If you favor a particular major, you can use these definitions to detect possible errors in your notions about it. By contrasting the definition of *your* major with the descriptions of the others, you can sharpen your understanding of your discipline and see how it relates to those others. This information can help you select a minor as well as electives that can give you the flexibility you may be seeking in your studies.

Students frequently ask about the advantages and disadvantages of certain majors for securing a job. It would take half the pages in this book to cover the many aspects of this question — and the answer still would not be adequate. The personal factors that make a major suitable for you are much more important than the *current* market for jobs related to it.

Yes, we can say that Computer Science is the fastest growing major in colleges. It is also true that today it offers some of the highest starting salaries. But all this means little if you do not have the temperament, the interest, and the aptitudes that this field requires. If you don't possess the necessary attributes for computer science, you may have difficulty finding satisfactory work. And even if you do land a job, you may wind up unhappy and make little progress in it.

After all, your college major does not train you for one specific job. It seeks to develop your aptitudes and abilities so that you can use them with satisfaction and profit *in the broadest variety of careers.* That's why it is so important to choose a major which allows *your* individual talents to flourish. More people than you may realize find themselves trapped in well-paying jobs they would like to leave but can't, because their financial commitments do not permit them to take a more satisfying position that would at first pay a lot less money.

Even if we tried to evaluate majors in terms of today's market, it would be risky business. Choosing a major this way calls for predictions of what lies three to four years ahead. Who can predict that far ahead when even our most respected economists cannot agree whether interest rates will rise or fall in the next three months? Just a few years ago the prospects for engineering and teaching seemed dismal. Today engineers are in short supply and we are seeing reports of teacher shortages, at least in science, mathematics, and special education at this time.

This is not to say you can disregard the career implications of the studies you undertake and pay no attention to the ways you might improve the immediate marketability of your skills, no matter what major you choose. Whatever courses in computer science, management or accounting you can fit into your schedule will stand you in good stead. What's more, you will never regret any special efforts you make to develop your writing and speaking skills. Executives put these skills at the head of the list when they enumerate the qualities you need to succeed in business.

Especially when the economy is sluggish the best advice is to make your studies as flexible and wide-ranging as you can. This means that enlightened self-fulfillment is the best road to a reasonably happy existence. And the object is to achieve this fulfillment in a way that will also bring you the greatest financial reward.

Ultimately, what pays off is how well you appraise yourself and find ways to discover, develop, and use your skills and capabilities. The most important thing about your education is how well it suits *you* and what *you* creatively do with it.

CAREER LEADS

Each specific major in this book has a section that lists *Career Leads*. These leads include some of the occupations graduates of that major went into, as well as other jobs related to that area of study. You can use these leads to expand your knowledge of the range of jobs connected to your major field, and to get a better grasp of your own likes and dislikes regarding occupations.

In almost every profession, there is room for people whose interest patterns and personalities vary. But job seekers often don't take so wide a view of occupations as they might, and sometimes fail to look beyond common stereotypes. For example, a common image of a lawyer is that of an outgoing, talkative person who enjoys addressing a jury. Many students do not realize that there are also lawyers who limit themselves to research, who write, or who hold full-time executive positions. Nor do people always recognize the value of an undergraduate major in pre-med, classics, or physics, as background for law studies. For instance, the study of anatomy can facilitate an attorney's grasp of a malpractice suit; classics gives one an understanding of the origins of a legal system; and physics can be helpful in the practice of patent law or litigations between large scientific corporations.

Other possibilities that students do not immediately think of for chemistry, accounting, or almost any other major, are jobs as editors of technical books and periodicals; art history majors seldom realize that banks and other financial institutions may need their skills to design brochures and other printed materials.

Using the Career Leads section, you can start your evaluation of career interests related to your major by checking off the occupations that appeal to you. List those careers with their six-digit numbers alongside. Then, underline the first three digits preceding the decimal which appear most often. These three digits will identify the occupational division you prefer. For example, if the first three numbers are 052, they indicate you prefer occupations in history; if 072, dentistry; if 143, occupations in photography.

Say, for example, that as an art history major you come up with 102 and 141 as the first three digits of the careers you prefer. For 102, you will find three listings under Career Leads, and for 141 you will find six. If you are interested in learning about additional careers in these two groups, you can then go to *The Dictionary of Occupational Titles*. There, under 102 — Museum Curators and Related Occupations — you will find a description of these eight different occupations:

102.017	Curator (museum)
102.117	Supervisor, historic sites
102.167	Art Conservator
102.261	Conservation Technician
102.261	Paintings Restorer
102.361	Restorer, Lace and Textiles (museum)
102.367	Fine Arts Packer
102.381	Museum Technician

In the same manner, under 141 — Commercial Artists: Designers and Illustrators, Graphic Arts — you will find 11 listings. This will enable you to see the much broader scope of options within the groups that attract you.

The Career Leads section of a particular major will sometimes point out a seemingly unrelated connection you might easily overlook. For instance, since you find a Dramatic Arts Historian under 052 — Occupations in History — in *The Dictionary of Occupational Titles*, it may lead you to explore additional occupations not only in history but also other fields such as anthropology, archeology, and ethnology in which your art history training might apply.

Once you have identified some of the jobs you like, you can make some finer distinctions about your preferences by referring to the second set of three numbers following the decimal.

As we explained in the section on the Meaning of Number and Letter Codes, these numbers tell you the degree to which a job requires you to work with data, people, and things. With this information, you can find which jobs are more compatible with your disposition. Assume, for example, that as an art history major you are interested in the 141 group of occupations,

---

and you select the following two of the 11 listed in the DOT.

		Data	People	Things
Illustrator	141.	0	6	1
Art Director	141.	0	3	1

You would find that an Illustrator is just as much involved as the Art Director with Data (0) and Things (1), but that the Art Director has a much higher degree of direct involvement with People, as the lower number indicates. This knowledge could help you decide which job you might wish to seek out first.

The last item of information related to the title of an occupation under Career Leads is the three-letter occupational code which we have also previously described under Meaning of Number and Letter Codes. This letter code gives you some idea of the personality traits of people in a particular job, as well as the outstanding features of its work environment. As you recall, there are six personality types: Realistic, Investigative, Artistic, Social, Enterprising, and Conventional (RIASEC).

In the above example, Illustrator and Art Director, the letter codes for both are AIS. This information allows you to look up all other AIS occupations found in this book — even if listed under other majors. This may help you discover not only new career leads but also supplementary courses that could assist you in rounding out your background.

Also, remember that these letter codes are not ironclad measures. They are merely *estimates* of the qualities they represent. For this reason, you may be able to locate other promising careers by looking for occupations that have various combinations of your letter code.

Whatever leads you decide to pursue, it will be worth your time to check out the precise nature of the work in *The Dictionary of Occupational Titles* and the *Occupational Outlook Handbook*, both of which are published by the United States Department of Labor. The DOT gives precise descriptions of each job, while the OOH gives some current assessment of the job market. Checking these books will help you avoid romantic illusions about a job that may in the end disappoint you. It will also prevent you from turning down a job on the basis of false notions you may have acquired about it. Frequently jobs you fear will "chain you to a desk," or jobs you want because you "like to work with people," turn out to be quite different from what you'd expected.

There is no quick or foolproof way of finding the right job for *you*. But whatever combination or sequence of methods you use, you are sure to increase your knowledge about careers and gain an awareness of *your* interests and needs. These insights can help you face your future with increasing self-assurance.

HIRING INSTITUTIONS

Here we present a variety of establishments that can use the training you acquired in your major field of study. Once you discover the wide range of fields available to you, this information will make you aware of the types of potential employers you might consider when looking for a job.

Some organizations identify so strongly with a particular product or service that we sometimes neglect to investigate the many other kinds of jobs they offer. For example, labor unions and corporations such as IBM need teachers for the many training and educational programs they conduct on their own premises. Hospitals, besides needing nurses and doctors, require social workers, librarians, and finance officers. Department stores use art history and English majors to design and write their many manuals and advertising copy.

Also, regardless of what they produce, the largest corporations employ almost every conceivable type of college graduate and professional. True, a high school may hire more teachers than the phone company, and the Internal Revenue Service may hire more accountants than a health club, but remember: You can fill only one job whether there are two or 22 openings. The trick is to be the best applicant for the one job you really want.

To get that one job which is best for you, once again, it will pay you to work hard at the self-assessment we have suggested for you. By doing this, you can find out which leads will be most profitable in meeting *your* needs and help you avoid chasing down blind alleys. You will have an edge if, as is likely, you discover unusual connections that take you off the beaten track.

In the course of evaluating your skills and interests, take account of the nature of the institutions and the details of jobs that interest you. Remember that hiring institutions — work environments — have their own personality traits just as you do. Determine those features which for you would be advantages or disadvantages.

For example, one job may require extensive travel and another may entail relocation to a Sunbelt State. If you like to travel, the first job would present an advantage. If you need a more stable and structured environment to function effectively, you might consider travel as a disadvantage. In the same way, the Sunbelt is a plus if you enjoy tanning yourself, but a minus if warm weather drains you, or if you like snow and ski slopes.

Other factors worth thinking about are the products or data you will handle and the types of people with whom you would have contact. As a sporting goods salesperson, for instance, you would spend much time in country clubs, health spas, or college recreation centers, while medical detailing for a pharmaceutical firm will take you to doctors' offices and hospitals. As an accountant, your social contacts would vary substantially if you worked for NBC-TV, the Carnegie Foundation, or the FBI. Nurses would have equally varied interpersonal experiences if they worked in a hospital, aboard a cruise ship, or at the Kennedy Space Center.

Since your work environment can have a profound influence on your social life, it will be helpful to know how pleasant conditions are likely to be for you. As a personnel officer who loves music but has a limited interest in sports, you would certainly be happier working for the Metropolitan Opera Company than at Madison Square Garden.

Finally, the size and the type of control that an employment establishment exercises can have consequences important for you to know about. For example, in a large corporation such as GE or IBM, there would be more opportunity to move up the ladder in your specialty. On the other hand, in a smaller corporation you can get a more diversified experience, which can broaden your options regarding areas to specialize in for the future.

Also, note how employment conditions differ in private industry, in government, and various kinds of non-profit organizations. Jobs with municipal, State, and Federal agencies tend to have more security than jobs in private industry, but at the same time are likely to be more rigid and bureaucratic. Then, too, government jobs, at all levels, unless they're on a civil service track, will last only as long as your political party remains in power.

In education, while salaries may lag behind those in business and industry, tenure gives you greater job security. In addition, you have much longer vacations which permit you to travel, to work on personal or professional projects, or to experiment with other types of work while supplementing your income at the same time.

Under the hiring institutions that interest you, jot down those features of the job or the institution which for *you* are advantages or disadvantages. Don't use guesswork. Get facts before you make a judgment about your preferences. Keep in mind that if the work environment suits your personality, chances are you will find congenial colleagues and co-workers there.

It will be worth your while to do this analysis before you start any serious job-hunting. If you do, you will greatly improve your chances of landing a job in which you can thrive and prosper.

CURRENT OCCUPATIONS OF GRADUATES

Under each major, we list the actual occupations graduates entered over a period of 20 years.

Under the heading *1975-80*, three columns list the jobs alumni got and the number of men and women, separately and combined, who entered them during the six-year period immediately following graduation. For recent graduates of each major, these columns provide leads to jobs which have been most available at the entry level. They also show the beginning jobs that are more readily available either to men or to women in cases where hiring practices may differ. This information can help new graduates concentrate their job seeking efforts in those areas where their search is more likely to prove successful.

In the column titled *1960-74*, we list the jobs held by graduates who completed college during this 15-year period. Since the graduates in this group have been in the job market at least seven, and in some cases as many as 20, years, we can view their present jobs as indicating long-term career possibilities for that major.

Once you identify the things you do well, that give you satisfaction, and that have meaning for you — the process we described under Self-Assessment — you can begin to investigate those occupations of former graduates that appeal to you. In exploring career possibilities, you will need current and accurate occupational information. You can get this through recent publications, from summer jobs or internships in which you can test your skills, and by visiting and talking to people who are in the positions that interest you. In addition to your own resourcefulness and ingenuity, high school Guidance Offices, Career Counseling Centers in colleges, libraries, or community agencies can help you get the information you need.

JOB INDEX
MAJOR OF GRADUATES BY OCCUPATION

In the Index, we list alphabetically the positions which alumni currently hold, as well as the DOT numbers and the Holland letter identification for each job. Then we indicate the number of graduates from each major who occupy those positions. Here again we have two categories of graduates (1960-74; 1975-80), with the latter group showing separately the jobs men and women occupy.

The subdivisions under the 1975-80 category enable men and women to find entry positions listed by sex as well as those listed under their major. And the reader can find from the 1960-74 listings careers that graduates of related majors have entered. These tabulations show that graduates of 16 different majors are computer programers, those of 11 different majors are in public relations and hospital administration, and each of these occupations includes majors in English, economics, history, psychology, and sociology. Students in any one of these five majors, for example, according to their interests, could take electives in computer science, writing, or business management to compete more effectively for one of these positions.

The variety of jobs students in the humanities occupy can serve to reinforce the fact that training in history, English, or philosophy need not restrict job opportunities to the field in which the major concentrates. Our listings show that history majors hold jobs in research and development, philosophy majors in social welfare work, and English majors in hospital administration. And the large number of majors which appear under many occupations should impress the reader with the adaptability of almost every undergraduate course of study. You will find it heartening to see that administrative officers, business executives, lawyers, social workers, and systems analysts have all come from at least 16 different majors.

There is still another way you can use the Index to help you select either a major or a career. If you already have a major, you can see in which job categories it can lead to the greatest number of employment opportunities. You will note, for example, that business and economics majors abound in market research positions, and English majors in editing and reporting. A variety of majors, in almost equal numbers, are real-estate agents or hospital administrators. And there are also some positions that just a few graduates with a particular major seem to enter. For some reason, you do not find many buyers who majored in English, or copy writers who studied science. This information will help you prepare to present yourself more astutely and creatively in seeking jobs which fewer people with your major have entered. It will also show you that there are not many jobs for which your major disqualifies you.

Should you already have a career in mind — such as personnel manager, lawyer, business executive, or physician —

the Index can help you in choosing a major (or suitable electives). The information it contains can be especially helpful if you prefer studies that do not have a direct or logical connection with the career you wish to pursue. For example, if you want to be a business executive or an administrative officer but prefer to study the humanities, would you prejudice your chances for success by majoring in history or English? Here the Index shows that although most business executives have studied business administration, they came from *all* majors —and at least 20 percent of them from the humanities. Similarly, while 55 percent of lawyers majored in history, economics, or political science, at least 20 percent majored in English, modern languages, philosophy, or classics.

Once you are aware of the range of studies which qualify you for the career you think you prefer, you will feel more secure about choosing the major for which you have the greatest interest and aptitude. You will then avoid the common pitfall of choosing an inappropriate major — a misstep that can result in poor performance and eventual withdrawal from college.

PART FOUR

CAREERS BY DEPARTMENTAL MAJOR

Any fact is better established by two or three good testimonies than by a thousand arguments.

— Emmons

The one thing that hurts more than paying an
income tax is not having to pay an income tax.
— Lord Dewar

ACCOUNTANCY
GENERAL DESCRIPTION

Accountants analyze business records and prepare financial reports such as balance sheets, cost studies, and tax statements. They also audit accounts for business, financial, and industrial firms, and install and maintain a general accounting system. The major areas they specialize in are public, managerial, and governmental accounting.

Public accountants have their own business, or work for accounting firms. They may specialize in areas such as auditing, taxes, or estate-planning. Management accountants, employed by individual firms, deal with many aspects of corporate operations such as auditing, budgeting, taxes, costs and investments. Government accountants examine records of Federal agencies and audit private businesses whose operations must comply with government regulations. They may also function as agents of the Internal Revenue Service or the Federal Bureau of Investigation.

It is becoming increasingly important for accountants to be familiar with computer programing and to understand how electronic data processing can apply to accounting operations. It is also essential for them to be effective in oral and written communication, because much of an accountant's work involves conveying and interpreting data for clients. Competent public accountants can become managers or partners within their company, or, as is often the case, transfer to executive positions in private firms and corporations.

A bachelor's degree qualifies you for entry jobs in this field. Undergraduate accounting internships and some computer training can also help in securing beginning positions. A Certified Public Accountant certificate — the C.P.A. — can greatly broaden your opportunities to advance in the accounting field.

CAREER LEADS

DOT	JOB TITLE	HOC
160.167	Accountant (budget, cost, systems)	CES
020.167	Actuary	IAS
188.117	Administrative officer/government service	ESC
160.162	Auditor	CES
186.117	Bank officer	ESC
161.117	Budget officer	CES
160.207	Budget consultant	CES
160.167	Bursar/education	CES
189.167	Business/management trainee	ESC
162.157	Buyer	ECS
213.132	Computer-operations supervisor	CIS
020.187	Computer programer	IAS
186.117	Controller	ESC
191.267	Credit analyst	ESC
168.167	Credit-and-collection manager	SIE
169.167	Data processing manager	ESC
090.167	Department head, college	SIA
020.167	Financial analyst	IAS
187.117	Hospital administrator	SEC
109.067	Information scientist	IRC
250.257	Insurance agent/broker	ECS
168.267	Internal-revenue investigator	SIE
110.107	Lawyer	ESA
161.167	Management analyst	CES
189.117	Manager, industrial organization	ESC
050.067	Market-research analyst	IAS
169.167	Office manager	ESC
184.117	Operations manager	ESC
162.157	Purchasing agent	ECS
186.117	Real-estate agent	ESC
250.357	Real-estate broker	ECS
186.167	Securities trader/banking	ESC
375.167	Special agent/FBI	SRE
251.157	Stockbroker	ECS
012.167	Systems analyst	ERI
160.162	Tax accountant	CES
110.117	Tax attorney	ESA

DOT	JOB TITLE	HOC
160.167	Tax auditor	CES
090.227	Teacher/college	SIA
091.227	Teacher/high school	SAE
184.187	Traffic manager	ESC
161.117	Treasurer	CES
166.167	Wage-and-salary administrator	SEC

HIRING INSTITUTIONS

Accounting Firms
Advertising Companies
Banks, Savings/Commercial
Booking Agencies
Business Corporations
Chain Stores
Civic and Taxpayers' Associations
Colleges and Schools
Construction Companies
Credit Unions
Educational Institutions
Financial Institutions
Government Agencies
Hospitals
Industries, Manufacturing
Insurance Companies
Internal-Revenue Service
Investment Firms
Labor Unions
Law Firms
Management Consulting Firms
Marketing-Research Departments and Firms
Nursing Homes
Philanthropic Associations
Publishers
Radio/Television Stations
Real Estate Companies

Research-and-Development Firms
Retail Stores
Talent Booking Agencies
Tax-Consulting Firms
Trade Associations
Utility Companies

CURRENT OCCUPATIONS OF GRADUATES
WHO MAJORED IN ACCOUNTANCY

DOT	JOB TITLE	HOC	1960-1974	1975-1980 M	F	T
160.167	Accountant	CES	249	218	50	268
160.167	Accounting manager	CES	41	11	3	14
160.167	Accounting partner	CES	17	4		4
188.117	Administrative officer/ government service	ESC	9			
164.117	Advertising manager	AES	2			
— —	Armed services	—	16	2	1	3
160.162	Auditor	CES	69	40	7	47
186.117	Bank officer	ESC	24	9	6	15
183.117	Branch manager	ESC	1	3		3
186.117	Brokerage-house partner	ESC			1	1
161.117	Budget analyst	CES	7	2	1	3
189.117	Business executive	ESC	113	7		7
162.157	Buyer	ECS	1	1		1
186.117	Cashier, bank	ESC			1	1
120.007	Clergy	SAI	1	1		1
209.562	Clerk	CIE	5	8	4	12
213.362	Computer operator	CIS	1			
213.132	Computer-operations supervisor	CIS	6	1		1
020.187	Computer programer	IAS	2	4	1	5
869.664	Construction worker	REI	1			
160.167	Cost accountant	CES	13	7	1	8
160.267	Cost estimator	CES	1			
191.267	Credit analyst	ESC	2	2		2
168.167	Credit-and-collection manager	SIE	2	1	1	2

DOT	JOB TITLE	HOC	1960-1974	1975-1980 M	F	T
003.161	Development-and-planning engineer	IRE	2			
110.117	District attorney	ESA	1			
183.117	District manager	ESC	2	2		2
050.067	Economist/price	IAS	1			
828.261	Field engineer	RIC	1			
020.167	Financial/investment analyst	IAS	27		1	1
050.067	Financial planner	IAS	18	8	1	9
373.364	Firefighter	RSE		1		1
189.117	General manager	ESC	28	4	1	5
— —	Graduate student	—	3	2		2
045.107	Guidance counselor	SIA	2			
091.107	High-school official	SAE	2			
187.117	Hospital administrator	SEC	4			
250.257	Insurance agent/broker	ECS	7	1		1
241.217	Insurance-claim adjuster	CSE	1			
168.267	Insurance-claim examiner	SIE	1			
169.167	Insurance underwriter	ESC	2		1	1
376.367	Investigator	SRE	1			
166.167	Labor-relations consultant	SEC	1			
— —	Law student	—		2		2
110.107	Lawyer	ESA	18			
230.367	Mail carrier	CSR		2		2
012.167	Management/methods engineer	ERI	1			
189.167	Management trainee	ESC	2	2	1	3
163.117	Marketing manager	ESC	2			
050.067	Marketing-research analyst	IAS	3			
— —	Medical student	—		1		1
152.047	Music director	ASI	1			
152.041	Musician	ASI	1			
169.167	Office manager	ESC	21	1		1
184.167	Operations manager	ESC	8	2	1	3
166.117	Personnel manager	SEC	3	1		1
375.263	Police officer	SRE	1	1		1
189.117	Private-business owner	ESC	10	2		2
189.117	Product manager	ESC	5	1		1

DOT	JOB TITLE	HOC	1960-1974	1975-1980		
---	---	---	---	M	F	T
183.117	Production manager	ESC		1		1
162.157	Purchasing agent	ECS	1		1	1
250.357	Real-estate agent/ broker	ECS	2	1		1
160.167	Revenue agent	CES	22	3		3
290.477	Sales clerk	ESC	1	2		2
290.477	Sales manager	ESC	2	2		2
279.357	Sales/service representative	ESC	2	2		2
186.167	Securities trader	ESC	1			
186.167	Security officer	ESC		1		1
600-800	Skilled trades	RIC		2	1	3
195.107	Social worker	SIC	1			
375.167	Special agent/FBI	SRE	6	1		1
251.157	Stockbroker	ECS	1	2		2
185.167	Store manager	ESI	1	1		1
070.101	Surgeon	ISA	1			
012.167	Systems analyst/electronic data processing	ERI	8			
160.162	Tax accountant	CES	18	10	1	11
160.167	Tax administrator	CES	6	2		2
110.117	Tax attorney	ESA	6			
090.227	Teacher/college	SIA	2			
091.227	Teacher/high school	SAE	7			
099.227	Teacher/other	SIR	1	1		1
159.147	Television/radio personnel	AES		1		1
184.117	Traffic analyst/manager	ESC	1	1		1
186.117	Trust officer/bank	ESC		1		1
073.101	Veterinarian	IRS	1			
			854	388	86	474

Every artist dips his brush in his own soul, and
paints his own nature into the pictures.
                    — Henry Ward Beecher

ART HISTORY
GENERAL DESCRIPTION

T he art historian examines the significant achievements of artists, architects, and musicians to determine how their works have contributed to the development of culture. In this program students analyze and evaluate many forms of artistic expression, such as painting, sculpture, architecture, music, and cinematography.

Work-leads related to art history include teaching, lecturing, writing criticism or biographies of artists and performers. An art-history specialist can also serve as consultant to publishers, and to radio, TV, and movie producers, or function as a museum curator, copy writer, layout designer, or historic-preservationist.

Students with a bachelor's degree in art history can get beginning jobs in advertising and publishing firms, museums, educational institutions, and government agencies. They can also find employment in many types of business establishments where their training qualifies them to perform tasks related to interior and industrial design, buying, and advertising.

Art history can serve as background for additional studies —or in some cases apprenticeships — in medical illustration, photo-engraving, fashion design, or audiovisual technology. More responsible positions in museums or colleges and universities usually call for advanced degrees.

CAREER LEADS

DOT	JOB TITLE	HOC
763.381	Antiquer, furniture	RIC
191.287	Appraiser, art	ESC
001.061	Architect	AIR
101.167	Archivist	SAI
294.257	Art auctioneer	ESC
102.167	Art conservator/museum	AEI
131.067	Art critic	ASI
141.031	Art director	ASI
149.021	Art teacher	ASI
076.127	Art therapist	SIR
191.117	Artist's manager	ESC
188.117	Arts-and-Humanities-Council, director	ESC
191.117	Booking agent	ESC
018.261	Cartographic technician	RCI
141.061	Cartoonist	ASI
141.051	Color expert	ASI
970.381	Colorist/photography	AIR
141.081	Commercial designer (books, albums)	ASI
055.381	Conservator, artifacts	IAR
131.067	Critic (art, drama, film)	ASI
102.017	Curator (art galleries, museums)	AEI
142.061	Designer (banknote, textiles, furniture)	AIS
142.061	Designer (display, fashion, industrial, set, stage)	AIS
159.147	Disc jockey	AES
142.031	Display manager	AIS
142.081	Floral designer	AIS
141.061	Graphic designer	ASI
052.067	Historian/dramatic arts	SEI
141.061	Illustrator/medical and scientific	ASI
142.051	Interior designer	AIS
700.281	Jeweler	RIC
141.061	Layout artist	ASI
100.127	Librarian	SAI
191.117	Literary agent	ESC
131.067	Movie critic	ASI
102.381	Museum technician	AEI

DOT	JOB TITLE	HOC
131.067	Music critic	ASI
142.081	Package designer	AIS
144.061	Painter/sculptor	AIR
102.261	Paintings restorer	AEI
143.062	Photographer	AIR
144.061	Printmaker	AIR
109.267	Research assistant (documents and records)	IRC
277.457	Salesperson/art objects	ESC
142.061	Set decorator	AIS
142.061	Set designer (motion pictures, radio, TV)	AIS
017.281	Technical illustrator	RIA

HIRING INSTITUTIONS

Advertising Departments and Firms
Architectural Firms
Art Galleries
Business Corporations
Colleges and Schools
Community Organizations
    YM-YWCAs
    YM-YWHAs
    Scouts, etc.
Construction Firms
Department Stores
Educational Institutions
Engineering Firms
Film Companies
Furniture Manufacturers
Garment Industry
Government Agencies
Historical Societies
Insurance Companies
Interior-Design Companies
Libraries

Magazines
Motion-Picture Companies
Museums
National and State Parks
Pharmaceutical Companies
Photography Studios
Planetariums
Publishing Companies
Radio/Television Stations
Research Organizations
Restoration Firms
Textile Manufacturers

CURRENT OCCUPATIONS OF GRADUATES WHO MAJORED IN ART HISTORY

DOT	JOB TITLE	HOC	1960-1974	1975-1980 M	F	T
188.117	Administrative officer/ government service	ESC	1			
144.061	Artist	AIR	2			
099.167	Audiovisual specialist	SIE	1			
189.117	Business executive	ESC	1	1		1
162.157	Buyer	ECS	1			
120.007	Clergy member	SAI	1			
209.562	Clerk	CIE			1	1
090.117	College/university official	SIA			1	1
— —	Graduate student	—	1		1	1
045.107	Guidance counselor	SIA			1	1
110.107	Lawyer	ESA			1	1
189.117	Research/development director	ESC		1		1
290.477	Sales clerk	ESC	1			
195.107	Social worker	SIC	1			
003.167	Systems engineer	IRE	1			
090.227	Teacher/college	SIA	2			
092.227	Teacher/elementary	SAI			1	1
091.227	Teacher/high school	SAE	3			
184.117	Traffic analyst/manager	ESC			1	1
			16	2	7	9

*Whenever you examine an animal closely, you feel
as if a human being inside were making fun of you.*
— *Elias Canetti*

BIOLOGY
GENERAL DESCRIPTION

Biology is the science of living matter. It involves the study of the structure, evolutionary development, and functions of plants, animals, and micro-organisms — especially the ways in which they relate to our environment.

Biologists specialize in many fields such as agronomy, anatomy, botany, embryology, genetics, horticulture, oceanography, pathology, physiology, or zoology. Even within these subdivisions, numerous subspecialties exist. Under botany, for example, we find plant scientists, such as taxonomists, phytopathologists, bryologists, and mycologists. And the field of applied biology, such as the biomedical sciences, includes pharmacology, nutrition, immunology, and pathology. Agriculture has subdivisions such as agronomy, animal husbandry, and seed technology.

Employment opportunities for biologists occur in business and industry with firms that produce agricultural chemicals, pest controls, dietary supplements, foods and beverages. Manufacturers of textiles, petroleum and leather goods offer other opportunities. Pharmaceutical houses throughout the United States employ biologists in large numbers. Biological training, plus talent and interest in literary and graphic arts, can lead to jobs in scientific illustration and writing.

Students with a bachelor's degree can do testing and inspecting in laboratories, and can also function as sales and service representatives in business and industry, or find beginning jobs with zoos, arboretums, museums and many government agencies. Teaching in colleges and universities, and more responsible research and administrative positions, require advanced degrees. Most holders of doctorates work in higher education, with smaller numbers in government and industry.

CAREER LEADS

DOT	JOB TITLE	HOC
029.081	Air-pollution analyst	IRA
041.061	Anatomist	IRS
041.061	Animal ecologist	IRS
040.061	Animal scientist	RIS
041.061	Biochemist	IRS
143.362	Biological photographer	AIR
041.061	Biologist	IRS
019.061	Biomedical engineer	RIE
041.061	Biophysicist	IRS
041.061	Botanist	IRS
079.101	Chiropractor	SIR
029.281	Criminologist	IRA
102.017	Curator	AEI
102.017	Curator/medical museum	AEI
102.017	Curator/zoological museum	AEI
041.061	Cytologist	IRS
078.281	Cytotechnologist	ISR
072.101	Dentist	ISR
077.117	Dietitian	SIE
077.061	Dietitian/research	SIE
132.017	Editor (technical and scientific publications)	ASI
041.061	Entomologist	IRS
029.081	Environmental analyst	IRA
029.081	Environmental scientist	IRA
168.267	Food-and-drugs inspector	SIE
070.061	Forensic pathologist	ISA
040.061	Forester	RIS
041.061	Geneticist	IRS
041.061	Histopathologist	IRS
187.117	Hospital administrator	SEC
024.061	Hydrologist	IRA
079.161	Industrial hygienist	SIR
109.067	Information scientist	IRC
199.364	Laboratory assistant	ICR
110.107	Lawyer	ESA
041.061	Marine biologist	IRS

DOT	JOB TITLE	HOC
141.061	Medical illustrator	ASI
100.167	Medical librarian	SAI
078.361	Medical technologist	ISR
041.061	Microbiologist	IRS
102.381	Museum technician	AEI
041.061	Mycologist	IRS
041.061	Nematologist	IRS
078.361	Nuclear medical technologist	ISR
168.167	Occupational-safety-and-health inspector	SIE
024.061	Oceanographer	IRA
079.101	Optometrist	SIR
071.101	Osteopath	ISR
041.061	Parasitologist	IRS
070.061	Pathologist	ISA
262.157	Pharmaceutical detailer	ESR
074.161	Pharmacist	IES
041.061	Pharmacologist	IRS
076.121	Physical therapist	SIR
070.101	Physician	ISA
041.061	Plant pathologist	IRS
041.061	Plant physiologist	IRS
079.101	Podiatrist	SIR
045.107	Psychologist/industrial	SIA
079.117	Public-health educator	SIR
168.264	Safety inspector	SIE
012.167	Safety manager	ERI
262.357	Sales representative (chemicals and drugs)	ESR
079.117	Sanitarian	SIR
195.107	Social worker	SIC
040.061	Soil scientist	RIS
199.261	Taxidermist	ICR
090.227	Teacher/college	SIA
091.227	Teacher/high school	SAE
073.101	Veterinarian	IRS
073.061	Veterinarian/laboratory animal care	IRS
131.267	Writer/technical, scientific	ASI
041.061	Zoologist	IRS

HIRING INSTITUTIONS

Advertising Agencies
Aquariums
Arboretums
Beverage Companies
Botanical Gardens
Chemical Industries
Colleges and Schools
Consulting Firms
Cosmetic Companies
Doctors' Offices
Educational Institutions
Food Processors
Government Agencies
      Agriculture Department
      Energy Department
      Environmental Protection Agency
      Fish and Wildlife Service
      Health and Human Services Department
      National Institutes of Health
      National Science Foundation
      Patent Office
      Peace Corps
      Vista
Hatcheries
Hospitals
Libraries, Medical/Technical
Lumber Companies
Medical Clinics
Medical Laboratories
Medical-Supply Companies
Museums
National and State Parks
Nurseries
Pharmaceutical Companies
Professional and Technical Journals
Publishers
Research-and-Development Firms
Textile Manufacturers
Zoological Parks

CURRENT OCCUPATIONS OF GRADUATES
WHO MAJORED IN BIOLOGY

DOT	JOB TITLE	HOC	1960-1974	1975-1980 M	F	T
160.167	Accountant	CES	1	1		1
150.047	Actor	ASE		1		1
070.101	Anesthesiologist	ISA	1			
— —	Armed services	—	13	2		2
041.061	Biochemist	IRS	1	1		1
041.061	Biologist	IRS	3	1		1
189.117	Business executive	ESC	1	2		2
189.167	Business/management trainee	ESC			1	1
022.161	Chemical-laboratory supervisor	IAR		1		1
022.061	Chemist	IAR	5	3	2	5
022.061	Chemist/analytical	IAR	2		2	
022.061	Chemist/quality control	IAR	1	1	1	2
022.061	Chemist/research	IAR	3	1	1	2
079.101	Chiropractor	SIR	1	1		1
120.007	Clergy member	SAI	1			
209.562	Clerk	CIE	2	2	2	4
090.117	College/university official	SIA	1			
020.187	Computer programer	IAS	2	1	2	3
869.664	Construction worker	REI		1		1
094.117	Coordinator of special services/education	SAI	1			
— —	Dental student	—	2	4		4
072.101	Dentist	ISR	35	3	1	4
092.137	Elementary-school official	SAI	1			
041.061	Endocrinologist	IRS	1			
189.117	General manager	ESC	2			
— —	Graduate student	—	20	22	10	32
091.107	High-school official	SAE	1			
040.061	Horticulturist	RIS	1			
187.117	Hospital administrator	SEC	3			
168.267	Insurance-claim examiner	SIE	1			
029.261	Laboratory technician	IRA	5	9	2	11
— —	Law student	—		2		2
110.107	Lawyer	ESA	2			

DOT	JOB TITLE	HOC	1960-1974	1975-1980 M	F	T
012.167	Management/methods engineer	ERI	1			
189.167	Management trainee	ESC			1	1
163.117	Marketing manager	ESC	1			
— —	Medical student	—	24	40	18	58
078.261	Medical technologist	ISR	2	1	2	3
041.061	Microbiologist	IRS	2	1	1	2
070.101	Obstetrician	ISA	8			
169.167	Office manager	ESC	1			
070.101	Ophthalmologist	ISA	7			
079.101	Optometrist	SIR	1			
070.101	Pediatrician	ISA	12	1		1
166.117	Personnel manager	SEC	1			
074.161	Pharmacist	IES	2			
— —	Pharmacy student	—	1			
070.101	Physician	ISA	98	7	2	9
079.101	Podiatrist	SIR	3			
— —	Podiatry student	—		2	1	3
189.117	Private-business owner	ESC	2			
163.267	Product-distribution manager		1		1	
183.117	Production manager	ESC	2			
070.107	Psychiatrist	ISA	7			
045.107	Psychologist	SIA	1			
070.101	Radiologist	ISA	8			
250.357	Real-estate agent/broker	ECS	1			
045.107	Rehabilitation counselor	SIA	1			
189.117	Research-and-development director	ESC	2	2	2	4
279.357	Sales/service representative	ESC	5	1	1	2
020.167	Securities analyst	IAS	1			
600-800	Skilled trades	RIC	1			
195.107	Social worker	SIC	1			
070.101	Surgeon	ISA	20			
012.167	Systems analyst/electronic data processing	ERI	1			
090.227	Teacher/college	SIA	9	1		1

DOT	JOB TITLE	HOC	1960-1974	1975-1980		
				M	F	T
092.227	Teacher/elementary school	SAI	1	1	1	2
091.227	Teacher/high school	SAE	17	5	3	8
099.227	Teacher/other	SIR	3	1		1
184.117	Transportation manager	ESC			1	1
070.101	Urologist	ISA	3			
073.101	Veterinarian	IRS	1		1	1
			362	125	56	181

Water is H$_2$O, hydrogen two parts, oxygen one, but there is also a third thing that makes it water, and nobody knows what that is.
— *D.H. Lawrence*

CHEMISTRY
GENERAL DESCRIPTION

C hemists study the structure and make-up of substances, and the way their interaction changes and transforms them. In basic research, chemists investigate properties of matter and the laws that come into play when elements combine. Those in research and development create new products, such as vaccines and synthetics, and they find ways to apply new knowledge to such fields as nutrition, genetics, electronics, drugs, and environmental protection.

The more common specialties are: analytical chemistry (the structure and composition of substances), organic chemistry (living organisms and carbon compounds), inorganic chemistry (compounds other than organic), physical chemistry (transformation of energy). Often, by combining with other sciences, these specialties produce new offshoots such as biochemistry or chemical oceanography.

The largest number of chemists do research and development in business and industry, most often with chemical manufacturing companies. The next-highest sources of employment are colleges and universities, followed by local, State, and Federal government agencies.

Graduates with a bachelor's degree can get beginning jobs in analysis and testing, or in technical sales and services. With appropriate courses in education, they can qualify for high-school teaching positions. You generally need the Ph.D. to do research, to teach in colleges and universities, and to move up in administrative positions.

CAREER LEADS

DOT	JOB TITLE	HOC
029.081	Air-pollution analyst	IRA
019.061	Biomedical engineer	RIE
041.061	Biochemist	IRS
008.061	Chemical engineer	IRE
022.161	Chemical-laboratory chief	IAR
559.130	Chemical-processing-plant supervisor	RIC
022.061	Chemist (analytical, quality control, research)	IAR
022.061	Chemist/food	IAR
022.061	Chemist/pollution control	IAR
078.261	Chemistry technologist/medical service	ISR
029.281	Criminalist	IRA
029.281	Crime-laboratory analyst	IRA
102.017	Curator/natural history (museum)	AEI
072.101	Dentist	ISR
077.117	Dietitian	SIE
077.061	Dietitian/research	SIE
132.017	Editor (technical and scientific publications)	ASI
029.081	Environmental analyst	IRA
029.081	Environmental scientist	IRA
168.267	Food-and-drug inspector	SIE
187.117	Hospital administrator	SEC
024.061	Hydrologist	IRA
012.167	Industrial-health engineer	ERI
109.067	Information scientist	IRC
199.364	Laboratory assistant	ICR
029.261	Laboratory technician	IRA
022.281	Laboratory tester	IAR
189.117	Manager/industrial organization	ESC
141.061	Medical illustrator	ASI
100.167	Medical librarian	SAI
078.361	Medical technologist	ISR
078.361	Nuclear medical technologist	ISR
168.167	Occupational-safety-and-health inspector	SIE
024.061	Oceanographer	IRA
079.101	Optometrist	SIR

DOT	JOB TITLE	HOC
071.101	Osteopath	ISR
110.117	Patent attorney	ESA
022.161	Perfumer	IAR
262.157	Pharmaceutical detailer	ESR
074.161	Pharmacist	IES
041.061	Pharmacologist	IRS
022.061	Physical chemist	IAR
070.101	Physician	ISA
029.281	Police chemist	IRA
183.117	Production manager	ESC
079.117	Public-health educator	SIR
012.167	Quality-control supervisor	ERI
012.167	Safety manager	ERI
262.357	Sales representative (chemicals and drugs)	ESR
079.117	Sanitarian	SIR
040.061	Soil scientist	RIS
090.227	Teacher/college	SIA
091.227	Teacher/high school	SAE
073.101	Veterinarian	IRS
029.081	Water-quality analyst	IRA
131.267	Writer, technical/scientific	ASI

HIRING INSTITUTIONS

Beverage Companies
Business Corporations
Chemical Industries
Colleges and Schools
Consulting Firms
Cosmetic Companies
Distributors of Scientific Equipment
Doctors' Offices
Educational Institutions
Engineering Firms
Food-Product Companies

Government Agencies
    Agriculture Department
    Consumer-Affairs Office
    Consumer Product Safety Commission
    Education Department
    Energy Department
    Environmental Protection Agency
    Fish and Wildlife Service
    Health and Human Services Department
    National Park Service
    National Science Foundation
    Patent Office
    Peace Corps
    Vista
Hospitals
Import/Export Companies
Industries, Manufacturing
Libraries, Medical/Technical
Lumber Companies
Manufacturing-and-Processing Firms
Medical Clinics
Medical Laboratories
Medical-Supply Companies
Mining Companies
Newspapers and Magazines
Paper Manufactuers
Petroleum Companies
Pharmaceutical Companies
Professional/Technical Journals
Publishers
Research-and-Development Firms
Textile Manufacturers
Utility Companies

CURRENT OCCUPATIONS OF GRADUATES
WHO MAJORED IN CHEMISTRY

DOT	JOB TITLE	HOC	1960-1974	1975-1980 M	F	T
188.117	Administrative officer/ government service	ESC	2			
— —	Armed services	—	7			
183.117	Branch manager	ESC	1			
189.117	Business executive	ESC	5		1	1
022.061	Chemist	IAR	33	4	3	7
022.061	Chemist/analytical	IAR	2			
022.061	Chemist/quality control	IAR	1			
022.061	Chemist/research	IAR	18			
120.007	Clergy member	SAI		1		1
090.117	College/university official	SIA	1			
213.132	Computer-operations supervisor	CIS	1			
020.187	Computer programer	IAS	1			
094.117	Coordinator of special services/education	SAI	1			
— —	Dental student	—		2		2
072.101	Dentist	ISR	5			
183.117	District manager	ESC	2			
092.137	Elementary-school official	SAI	1			
189.117	General manager	ESC	1			
— —	Graduate student	—	10	3	3	6
187.117	Hospital administrator	SEC		1		1
022.137	Laboratory supervisor	IAR	2			
029.261	Laboratory technician	IRA	1			
— —	Law student	—	1	1		1
110.107	Lawyer	ESA	1			
163.117	Marketing manager	ESC	5			
050.067	Market-research analyst	IAS	1			
— —	Medical student	—	3	7	1	8
041.061	Microbiologist	IRS	1			
169.167	Office manager	ESC	2			
070.101	Ophthalmologist	ISA	1			
110.117	Patent attorney	ESA	1			
041.061	Pharmacologist	IRS	1			
070.101	Physician	ISA	12	1		1

DOT	JOB TITLE	HOC	1960-1974	1975-1980		
				M	F	T
189.117	Private-business owner	ESC	2			
189.117	Product manager	ESC	4			
183.117	Production manager	ESC	3			
162.157	Purchasing agent	ECS	7			
012.167	Quality-control engineer	ERI	1			
070.101	Radiologist	ISA	1			
250.357	Real-estate agent/broker	ECS	1			
189.117	Research-and-development director	ESC	6			
160.167	Revenue agent	CES	1			
290.477	Sales clerk	ESC	1			
163.167	Sales manager	ESC	2			
279.357	Sales/service representative	ESC	6	1		1
012.167	Systems analyst/electronic data processing	ERI	1			
090.227	Teacher/college	SIA	8			
091.227	Teacher/high school	SAE	5			
099.227	Teacher/other	SIR	2	1		1
			175	22	8	30

Poetry heals the wounds inflicted by reason.
— *Novalis*

CLASSICS
GENERAL DESCRIPTION

In this major, people study the languages and civilization of the ancient Greek and Roman worlds. More specifically, students examine and evaluate the literary, intellectual, and artistic works of the authors, scholars, and artists of classical antiquity.

The study of the languages and the literary and art forms of antiquity lays bare the ideas and systems of communication that gave rise to our contemporary civilization, and in this way provides a background which you can apply in the arts, business, industry, the media, the professions, and education. Verbal and analytical skills deriving from classical studies qualify graduates for managerial and executive positions. You can also use the insights you acquire about human behavior in personnel work, or in educational and training activities for corporations, unions and social agencies. Your knowledge of the art and history of antiquity can lead to job opportunities in museums, art galleries, radio, television, and the theatre. And students who develop their writing and research skills will find that popular and learned magazines, newspapers, book publishers, and TV stations can use their services.

Persons with a bachelor's degree often find jobs in secondary school teaching or in business and finance. Additional training in the sciences, or in fields such as art, journalism, or library science can expand your job horizons. Those who continue their studies on the graduate level frequently become college teachers or lawyers.

CAREER LEADS

DOT	JOB TITLE	HOC
055.067	Anthropologist	IAR
055.067	Archeologist	IAR
101.167	Archivist	SAI
052.067	Biographer	SEI
131.067	Book critic	ASI
100.387	Cataloger	SAI
120.007	Clergy member	SAI
090.117	College/university official	SIA
139.087	Crossword-puzzle maker	ASI
102.017	Curator (art galleries, museums)	AEI
090.167	Department head, college/university	SIA
090.167	Director of institutional research	SIA
132.067	Editor/publications	ASI
132.067	Editor/dictionary	ASI
132.067	Editor/greeting card	ASI
132.267	Editorial assistant	ASI
131.067	Editorial writer	ASI
352.367	Flight attendant	ESA
131.267	Foreign correspondent	ASI
188.117	Foreign-service officer	ESC
055.067	Historical archeologist	IAR
184.117	Import/export agent	ESC
059.267	Intelligence specialist	SIA
051.067	International-relations specialist	SIA
110.107	Lawyer	ESA
100.127	Librarian	SAI
165.017	Lobbyist	AES
189.167	Management trainee	ESC
132.267	Manuscript reader (printing and publishing)	ASI
102.381	Museum technician	AEI
059.067	Philologist	SIA
209.387	Proofreader	CIE
109.267	Research assistant (documents and records)	IRC
277.357	Salesperson/books	ESC
059.067	Scientific linguist	SIA

DOT	JOB TITLE	HOC
131.087	Script reader	ASI
132.037	Story editor	ASI
090.227	Teacher/college	SIA
119.287	Title examiner	ESA
353.167	Tour guide	SRE
137.267	Translator	ASI
252.157	Travel agent	ECS
131.067	Writer (prose, fiction, and nonfiction)	ASI
131.267	Writer/technical publications	ASI

HIRING INSTITUTIONS

Air, Bus, and Rail Lines
Archives
Art Galleries
Business Corporations
Colleges and Schools
Educational Institutions
Film Companies
Government Agencies
> Civil Rights Commission
> Education Department
> Environmental Protection Agency
> Federal Trade Commission
> Government Printing Office
> Health and Human Services Department
> Labor Department
> Library of Congress
> National Labor Relations Board

Historical Societies
Import/Export Companies
Learned Periodicals
Libraries
Magazines
Museums
Newspapers
Publishing Companies
Radio/Television Stations
Travel Agencies

CURRENT OCCUPATIONS OF GRADUATES
WHO MAJORED IN CLASSICS

DOT	JOB TITLE	HOC	1960-1974	1975-1980 M	F	T
150.047	Actor	ASE	1			
188.117	Administrative officer/ government service	ESC	2			
— —	Armed services	—	1			
160.162	Auditor	CES	1			
189.117	Business executive	ESC	2		1	1
090.117	College/university official	SIA	2			
020.187	Computer programer	IAS	1			
183.117	District manager	ESC	1			
132.067	Editor	ASI		1		1
050.067	Financial planner	IAS		1		1
189.117	General manager	ESC	1			
— —	Graduate student	—	4	1		1
045.107	Guidance counselor	SIA	1			
119.267	Law clerk	ESA	1			
— —	Law student	—	1	1		1
110.107	Lawyer	ESA	14	1		1
189.167	Management trainee	ESC			1	1
070.101	Physician	ISA	1			
160.167	Revenue agent	CES	1			
290.477	Sales clerk	ESC		1		1
163.167	Sales manager	ESC	2			
600-800	Skilled trades	RIC	2			
185.167	Store manager	ESI	1			
070.101	Surgeon	ISA	1			
012.167	Systems analyst/ electronic data processing	ERI	1			
090.227	Teacher/college	SIA	5			
092.227	Teacher/elementary school	SAI	3		1	1
091.227	Teacher/high school	SAE	7			
099.227	Teacher/other	SIR	1			
			58	6	3	9

Economy is in itself a source of great revenue.
— *Seneca*

ECONOMICS
GENERAL DESCRIPTION

Economics is the study of how society uses its valuable resources to produce, distribute, and consume goods and services. Economists analyze the structure of institutions such as banks, the stock market, and labor unions. People trained in economics also deal with problems arising from inflation, unemployment, labor negotiations, taxes, and international trade.

Theoretical economists develop statistical and mathematical models to explain what causes such conditions as inflation, unemployment or recessions. Applied economists investigate the implications of theories in fields such as energy, finance, transportation, or industrial production. They also serve as advisers to business firms, financial institutions, or labor unions, and analyze data and prepare reports for these clients.

Economists specialize in many fields: advanced economic theory, econometrics, economic history, international economics, and public finance among them. Even as specialists, they can improve their job prospects by getting some training in mathematical methods of analysis and computer science. And since economists often have to present their findings verbally and in writing, they need effective communications skills.

Business, research and finance organizations employ the largest numbers of economists. Majors in this field also find jobs in local, State and Federal government agencies, as well as in secondary schools and colleges. They can qualify, in addition, as financial reporters, technical writers, and public relations practitioners.

Graduates with a bachelor's degree can get positions in business and industry as management and sales trainees. With some courses in statistics and computer science, they can get jobs in market research as well.

Those graduates who go on for advanced studies can achieve more responsible positions in business, research, and consulting firms, with the possibility of rising to top executive positions. A substantial number of economics majors go on to law school. In colleges and universities, they need the Ph.D. to get promotions and tenure.

CAREER LEADS

DOT	JOB TITLE	HOC
188.117	Administrative officer/government service	ESC
164.117	Advertising manager	AES
160.162	Auditor	CES
186.117	Bank officer	ESC
131.067	Book critic	ASI
162.157	Broker's floor representative	ECS
160.207	Budget consultant	CES
186.117	Business manager/education	ESC
162.157	Buyer	ECS
241.217	Claim adjuster	CSE
191.167	Claim agent	ESC
241.267	Claim examiner	CSE
131.067	Columnist/commentator	ASI
050.067	Commodity-industry analyst	IAS
213.132	Computer-operations supervisor	CIS
020.187	Computer programer	IAS
003.167	Computer-systems engineer	IRE
169.207	Conciliator	ESC
188.117	Consumer-affairs director	ESC
096.121	Consumer-services consultant	SRI
191.267	Credit analyst	ESC
168.167	Credit-and-collection manager	SIE
090.167	Department head/college	SIA
090.167	Director of institutional research	SIA
166.117	Director/industrial relations	SEC
050.117	Director/employment research planning	IAS
189.117	Director/research and development	ESC
188.167	Director of vital statistics	ESC

DOT	JOB TITLE	HOC
188.167	District customs director	ESC
050.067	Economist (financial, industrial, labor)	IAS
132.037	Editor, trade journal	ASI
012.167	Efficiency expert	ERI
166.267	Employment interviewer	SEC
001.061	Environmental planner	AIR
186.167	Estate planner	ESC
169.267	Financial-aid counselor	ESC
020.167	Financial analyst	IAS
184.167	Flight-reservations manager	ESC
293.157	Fund raiser/nonprofit organization	ESC
165.117	Fund-raising director	AES
166.267	Hospital-insurance representative	SEC
184.117	Import-export agent	ESC
109.067	Information scientist	IRC
250.257	Insurance agent/broker	ECS
059.267	Intelligence specialist	SIA
168.267	Internal-revenue investigator	SIE
050.067	International-trade economist	IAS
166.267	Job analyst	SEC
166.167	Labor-relations representative	SEC
110.107	Lawyer	ESA
050.067	Labor economist	IAS
165.017	Lobbyist	AES
161.167	Management analyst	CES
187.117	Manager/chamber of commerce	SEC
186.117	Manager/financial institution	ESC
050.067	Market-research analyst	IAS
166.067	Occupational analyst	SEC
166.117	Personnel manager	SEC
166.167	Placement director	SEC
165.067	Public-relations representative	AES
162.157	Purchasing agent	ECS
197.167	Purser	REI
250.357	Real-estate agent/broker	ECS
131.267	Reporter	ASI
161.267	Reports analyst	CES

DOT	JOB TITLE	HOC
012.167	Safety manager	ERI
251.257	Sales agent/financial services	ECS
163.167	Sales manager	ESC
186.167	Securities trader/banking	ESC
375.167	Special agent/ FBI	SRE
020.167	Statistician	IAS
251.157	Stockbroker	ECS
012.167	Systems analyst/electronic data processing	ERI
090.227	Teacher/college	SIA
166.227	Training instructor	SEC
161.117	Treasurer	CES
186.117	Trust officer/bank	ESC
166.167	Wage-and-salary administrator	SEC

HIRING INSTITUTIONS

Advertising Departments and Firms
Banks, Savings/Commercial
Brokerage Houses
Business Corporations
Chambers of Commerce
Civic and Taxpayer Associations
Colleges and Schools
Consulting Firms
Consumer Organizations
Department Stores
Educational Institutions
Employment Agencies
Financial Institutions
Fund-Raising Firms
Government Agencies
        Agriculture Department
        Airports
        Civil Rights Commission
        Consumer-Affairs Office
        Energy Department

Federal Communications Commission
Federal Trade Commission
Health and Human Services Department
Housing and Urban Development
International Trade Commission
Labor Department
Peace Corps
Social Security Administration
Treasury Department
Vista

Industries, Manufacturing
Insurance Companies
Investment Firms
Labor Unions
Magazines, Newspapers
Management Consulting Firms
Market-Research-Departments and Firms
Nursing Homes
Personnel Departments
Pharmaceutical Companies
Political-Action Groups
Professional/Technical Journals
Public-Relations Firms
Publishers
Real Estate Firms
Research-and-Development Firms
Trade Associations
Utility Companies

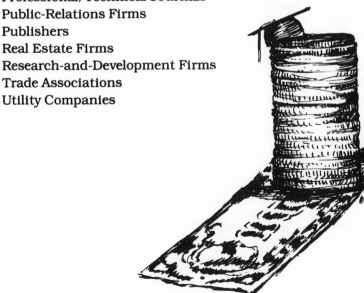

CURRENT OCCUPATIONS OF GRADUATES
WHO MAJORED IN ECONOMICS

DOT	JOB TITLE	HOC	1960-1974	1975-1980 M	F	T
160.167	Accountant	CES	15	5		5
160.167	Accounting manager	CES	4			
188.117	Administrative officer/ government service	ESC	20			
164.117	Advertising manager	AES	1			
— —	Armed services	—	24	1		1
160.161	Auditor	CES	8	1		1
186.117	Bank officer	ESC	47	2	1	3
183.117	Branch manager	ESC	3			
186.117	Brokerage-house partner	ESC	1			
161.117	Budget analyst	CES	4		1	1
189.117	Business executive	ESC	43	4		4
162.157	Buyer	ECS	2			
186.117	Cashier/bank	ESC	3			
022.061	Chemist	IAR		1		1
022.061	Chemist/quality control	IAR		1		1
110.117	Claim attorney	ESA	1			
120.007	Clergy member	SAI	1			
209.562	Clerk	CIE	3	3		3
090.117	College/university official	SIA	2			
213.362	Computer operator	CIS	2	1		1
213.132	Computer-operations supervisor	CIS	8	1		1
020.187	Computer programer	IAS	6	3		3
119.267	Contract consultant	ESA	2			
094.117	Coordinator of special services/education	SAI	2			
110.117	Corporate counsel	ESA	1			
160.167	Cost accountant	CES	1		1	1
160.267	Cost estimator	CES	2			
191.267	Credit analyst	ESC	2	2	1	3
168.167	Credit-and-collection manager	SIE	2	1		1
188.167	Customs officer	ESC	1			
003.167	Data-processing engineer	IRE	1			
003.167	Development-and-planning engineer	IRE	2			

DOT	JOB TITLE	HOC	1960-1974	1975-1980		
				M	F	T
110.117	District attorney	ESA	1			
183.117	District manager	ESC	9		1	1
050.067	Economist	IAS	6		1	1
003.061	Electrical engineer	IRE	2	1		1
020.167	Financial/investment analyst	IAS	15	1		1
050.067	Financial planner	IAS	4			
373.364	Firefighter	RSE		1		1
189.117	General manager	ESC	24	3		3
— —	Graduate student	—	14	1	1	2
045.107	Guidance counselor	SIA	4			
091.107	High school official	SAE	3			
187.117	Hospital administrator	SEC	4			
250.257	Insurance agent/broker	ECS	7			
241.217	Insurance-claim adjuster	CSE	1			
168.267	Insurance-claim examiner	SIE	4			
186.117	Insurance-and-risk manager	ESC	1			
169.167	Insurance underwriter	ESC	3	2		2
376.367	Investigator	SRE	2			
111.107	Judge	ESA	1			
022.137	Laboratory supervisor	IAR	1			
119.267	Law clerk	ESA	1			
— —	Law student	—	3	2		2
110.107	Lawyer	ESA	38			
100.127	Librarian	SAI	1			
230.367	Mail carrier	CSR	1			
189.167	Management trainee	ESC	2	1	1	2
163.117	Marketing manager	ESC	2			
050.067	Market-research analyst	IAS	10	1		1
078.261	Medical technologist	ISR	1			
131.267	Newspaper reporter	ASI	1			
169.167	Office manager	ESC	8	1		1
184.167	Operations manager	ESC	2			
195.167	Parole/probation officer	SIC	2			
166.117	Personnel manager	SEC	9	1		1
074.161	Pharmacist	IES	2			

DOT	JOB TITLE	HOC	1960-1974	1975-1980		
				M	F	T
070.101	Physician	ISA	1			
375.263	Police officer	SRE	4			
189.117	Private-business owner	ESC	7			
189.117	Product manager	ESC	3			
183.117	Production manager	ESC	2	1		1
045.107	Psychologist	SIA	2			
165.067	Public-relations practitioner	AES	2			
162.157	Purchasing agent	ECS	3			
012.167	Quality-control-engineer	ERI	1			
250.357	Real-estate agent/ broker	ECS	1			
045.107	Rehabilitation counselor	SIA	1			
160.167	Revenue agent	CES	4			
290.477	Sales clerk	ESC	7			
163.167	Sales manager	ESC	8			
279.357	Sales/service representative	ESC	28	1		1
020.167	Securities analyst	IAS	5			
186.167	Securities trader	ESC	2	1		1
189.167	Security officer	ESC	1			
600-800	Skilled trades	RIC	2			
188.117	Social-welfare director	ESC	1			
195.107	Social worker	SIC	2	1		1
375.167	Special agent/FBI	SRE	4			
020.067	Statistician	IAS	1			
251.157	Stockbroker	ECS	2			
185.167	Store manager	ESI	1			
070.101	Surgeon	ISA	1			
012.167	Systems analyst/electronic data processing	ERI	8	2		2
003.167	Systems engineer	IRE	2			
160.162	Tax accountant	CES	1	1		1
160.167	Tax administrator	CES	1	1		1
110.117	Tax attorney	ESA	1			
090.227	Teacher/college	SIA	7			
092.227	Teacher/elementary school	SAI	8	2	1	3
091.227	Teacher/high school	SAE	14			

DOT	JOB TITLE	HOC	1960-1974	1975-1980		
				M	F	T
099.227	Teacher/other	SIR	2			
159.147	Television/radio personnel	AES	1			
184.117	Traffic analyst/manager	ESC	2	1		1
166.227	Training specialist	SEC	1			
184.117	Transportation manager	ESC	1			
186.117	Trust officer/bank	ESC	7			
199.167	Urban planner	ICR	2			
131.267	Writer/technical	ASI	1			
			558	**52**	**9**	**61**

What's done to children, they will do to society.
— *Karl Menninger*

EDUCATION
GENERAL DESCRIPTION

Education deals with methods of instruction which promote human development and learning. Although most graduates begin their careers in education as teachers, nearly half of the 5,000,000 persons working in this field do administrative and personnel work, or they supply technical and supportive services.

The employment situation continues to be rather competitive, although opportunities in special education, pre-school education, and the teaching of science, industrial arts, and vocational subjects have continued to emerge. But now warnings are sounding from several sources that teacher shortages have begun to develop. The National Center for Educational Statistics, for one, predicts a growth of 13.7 percent in elementary enrollment by the end of this decade and projects that long before then — by 1986 — barely one teacher will be available for every teaching vacancy. In addition, the National Council for Accreditation of Teacher Education expects this anticipated shortage to become more critical in the late 1980's.

While waiting to get teaching jobs, graduates often find other positions which draw on the skills they have acquired by studying communications, administrative planning, training and motivating of young people, and learning-theory. Such positions involve personnel work, employment interviewing, job-training in unions and industry, employee educational-counseling in large corporations, as well as planning work with travel and recreational establishments.

A bachelor's degree is sufficient for achieving certification. Many states, however, require teachers to take courses in continuing education to maintain their skills. One usually needs additional degrees for salary-scale advances or for more responsible administrative posts.

CAREER LEADS

DOT	JOB TITLE	HOC
193.162	Air-traffic controller	RIE
090.117	Alumni secretary	SIA
153.227	Athletic coach	SRE
090.117	Athletic director/education	SIA
076.101	Audiologist	SIR
099.167	Audiovisual specialist	SIE
186.117	Business manager/education	ESC
099.167	Certification-and-selection specialist	SIE
188.117	Consumer-affairs director	ESC
096.121	Consumer-services consultant	SRE
188.117	Council-on-Aging director	ESC
045.107	Counselor (guidance, rehabilitation, vocational)	SIA
090.167	Department head, college/university	SIA
077.117	Dietitian	SIE
090.167	Director of admissions	SIA
090.167	Director of institutional research	SIA
090.167	Director of student affairs	SIA
099.117	Educational-program director	SIE
099.117	Education supervisor/correctional institution	SIE
094.227	Educational therapist	SAI
169.267	Financial-aid counselor	ESC
090.107	Foreign-student adviser	ESC
099.227	Instructor/correspondence school	SIE
153.227	Instructor/sports	SRE
100.127	Librarian	SAI
166.117	Personnel manager	SEC
166.167	Placement director	SEC
099.117	Principal/education	SIE
045.107	Psychologist/industrial	SIA
045.107	Psychologist/school	SIA
165.067	Public-relations representative	AES
162.157	Purchasing agent	ECS
195.167	Recreation director	SIC
090.167	Registrar, college/university	SIA

DOT	JOB TITLE	HOC
109.267	Research assistant	IRC
277.357	Salesperson/books	ESC
195.107	Social worker	SIC
076.107	Speech pathologist	SIR
099.227	Teacher/adult education	SIE
090.227	Teacher/college	SIA
092.227	Teacher/elementary school	SAI
094.227	Teacher/handicapped students	SAI
091.227	Teacher/high school	SAE
094.227	Teacher/mentally retarded	SAI
092.227	Teacher/preschool	SAI
166.227	Training instructor	SEC
099.227	Tutor	SIE

HIRING INSTITUTIONS

Adoption and Child Care Agencies
Boards of Education
Bookstores
Colleges and Schools
Community Organizations
    YM-YWCAs
    YM-YWHAs
    Scouts, etc.
Correctional Institutions
Day Care Centers
Educational Institutions
Educational Periodicals
Government Agencies
    Civil Rights Commission
    Consumer Affairs Office
    Education Department
    Environmental Protection Agency
    Federal Communications Commission
    Federal Labor Relations Authority
    Government Printing Office

Health and Human Services Department
Labor Department
Library of Congress
National Archives
Overseas Schools for Military Dependents
Peace Corps
Vista
Labor Unions
Libraries
Nursery Schools
Nursing Homes
Orphanages
Social-Service Agencies
Test-Development Corporations
Test-Preparation Institutes

CURRENT OCCUPATIONS OF GRADUATES WHO MAJORED IN EDUCATION

DOT	JOB TITLE	HOC	1960-1974	1975-1980 M	F	T
188.117	Administrative officer/ government service	ESC	1			
164.117	Advertising manager	AES			1	1
— —	Armed services	—	1			
189.117	Business executive	ESC	1		3	3
209.562	Clerk	CIE	1		8	8
090.117	College/university official	SIA	1		2	2
213.132	Computer-operations supervisor	CIS	1		1	1
020.187	Computer programer	IAS	1	1		1
094.117	Coordinator of special services/education	SAI	2	1		1
168.167	Credit-and-collection manager	SIE	1			
092.137	Elementary-school official	SAI	1		1	1
189.117	General manager	ESC	1		2	2
— —	Graduate student	—	2	1	1	2

DOT	JOB TITLE	HOC	1960-1974	1975-1980		
				M	F	T
045.107	Guidance counselor	SIA	1			
250.257	Insurance agent/broker	ECS	1			
241.217	Insurance-claim investigator	ESC		1		1
029.261	Laboratory technician	IRA	1			
— —	Law student	—		3	1	4
163.117	Marketing manager	ESC			1	1
078.261	Medical technologist	ISR	1			
166.117	Personnel manager	SEC	1			
375.263	Police officer	SRE	1			
189.117	Private-business owner	ESC	1			
189.117	Research-and-development director	ESC	1			
290.477	Sales clerk	ESC		1		1
163.167	Sales manager	ESC	1			
279.357	Sales/service representative	ESC	1		1	1
600-800	Skilled trades	RIC	3	2		2
195.107	Social worker	SIC	2			
375.167	Special agent/FBI	SRE	2	1		1
090.227	Teacher/college	SIA	1		1	1
092.227	Teacher/elementary school	SAI	81	4	60	64
091.227	Teacher/high school	SAE	7	8	8	16
099.227	Teacher/other	SIR	15	1	21	22
094.227	Teacher/special education	SAI	1	2	4	6
252.157	Travel agent	ECS	1		2	2
			137	26	118	144

The artistic temperament is a disease that afflicts amateurs. — *G.K. Chesterton*

ENGLISH
GENERAL DESCRIPTION

S tudents of English investigate the ways in which the written and spoken language takes form, and the techniques for using it effectively. They also evaluate the human response to experience as they find it expressed through literary art forms such as poetry, drama, and the novel. Such students develop theories of esthetics and methods of literary criticism which they apply in analyzing the major works of English and American literature.

Graduates who acquire the necessary skills can do entry-level writing, editing, research or production in the communications media. English majors with that kind of training can also get into public relations, advertising, or scientific-publishing jobs.

With this major, one can develop the ability to think clearly, interpret data, and communicate results, especially in writing. These skills can serve as a background for entry into many fields of human endeavor: business management, social work, library service, broadcasting, real estate, finance, and travel.

To function effectively, most businesses need employees who have good communications skills. English majors who master these skills can further increase their job prospects by taking business courses that attract them.

A bachelor's degree is usually sufficient for entry jobs in advertising, publishing, journalism, radio, TV, and government service, and trainee positions in business, industry, and finance. Graduates who go on to advanced studies frequently become lawyers, college professors, administrative officers and business executives.

CAREER LEADS

DOT	JOB TITLE	HOC
188.117	Administrative officer/government service	ESC
164.117	Advertising manager	AES
159.147	Announcer (radio and TV)	AES
191.287	Appraiser/art	ESC
101.167	Archivist	SAI
131.067	Art critic	ASI
191.117	Artist's manager	ESC
188.117	Arts-and-Humanities-Council director	ESC
132.137	Assignment editor (radio and TV)	ASI
186.117	Bank officer	ESC
052.067	Biographer	SEI
131.067	Book critic	ASI
120.007	Clergy	SAI
131.067	Columnist/commentator	ASI
020.187	Computer programer	IAS
131.087	Continuity writer	ASI
131.067	Copy writer/advertising	ASI
131.267	Correspondent	ASI
131.267	Critic (book, drama, film)	ASI
139.087	Crossword-puzzle maker	ASI
159.147	Disc jockey	AES
132.067	Editor/dictionary	ASI
132.067	Editor/greeting card	ASI
132.037	Editor/house organ	ASI
132.067	Editor/news	ASI
132.067	Editor/publications	ASI
132.037	Editor/trade journal	ASI
132.267	Editorial assistant	ASI
131.267	Editorial writer	ASI
131.267	Foreign correspondent	ASI
293.157	Fund raiser	ESC
165.117	Fund-raising director	AES
250.257	Insurance agent/broker	ECS
110.107	Lawyer	ESA
100.127	Librarian	SAI
191.117	Literary agent	ESC

DOT	JOB TITLE	HOC
189.167	Management trainee	ESC
132.267	Manuscript reader	ASI
131.067	Movie critic	ASI
131.267	Newscaster	ASI
131.267	Newswriter	ASI
209.387	Proofreader	CIE
165.067	Public-relations practitioner	AES
131.267	Reporter	ASI
109.267	Research assistant	IRC
131.267	Rewriter	ASI
277.357	Salesperson/books	ESC
259.357	Sales representative (radio and TV)	ECS
131.087	Script reader	ASI
375.167	Special agent/FBI	SRE
251.157	Stockbroker	ECS
132.037	Story Editor	ASI
090.227	Teacher/college	SIA
252.157	Travel agent	ECS
131.267	Writer/technical, scientific	ASI

HIRING INSTITUTIONS

Advertising Departments and Firms

Air, Bus, and Rail Lines

Banks, Savings/Commercial

Bookstores

Business Corporations

Colleges and Schools

Consumer Organizations

Department Stores

Educational Institutions

Film Companies

Fund-Raising Firms

Government Agencies

> Consumer Affairs Office
> Education Department
> Environmental Protection Agency
> Federal Trade Commission
> Government Printing Office
> Health and Human Services Department
> Labor Department
> Library of Congress
> National Foundation on the Arts and the Humanities
> Social Security Administration
> Vista

Industries, Manufacturing

Insurance Companies

Investment Firms

Labor Unions

Libraries

Literary Periodicals

Magazines and Newspapers

Personnel Departments

Political-Action Groups

Public-Relations Firms

Publishing Companies

Radio/Television Stations

Real Estate Firms

Research-and-Development Firms

Travel Agencies

Utility Companies

CURRENT OCCUPATIONS OF GRADUATES WHO MAJORED IN ENGLISH

DOT	JOB TITLE	HOC	1960-1974	1975-1980 M	F	T
160.167	Accountant	CES	1	1		1
160.167	Accounting manager	CES	1			
150.047	Actor	ASE	1	1		1
188.117	Administrative officer/ government service	ESC	8	2		2
164.117	Advertising manager	AES	1		2	2
— —	Armed services	—	19	2		2
144.061	Artist	AIR	1		1	1
186.117	Bank officer	ESC	6			
189.117	Business executive	ESC	29		2	2
162.157	Buyer	ECS	3	1		1
022.061	Chemist/quality control	IAR	1			
120.007	Clergy member	SAI	1			
209.562	Clerk	CIE	9	7	5	12
090.117	College/university official	SIA	6		1	1
213.362	Computer operator	CIS		1		1
213.132	Computer-operations supervisor	CIS	1			
020.187	Computer programer	IAS	1	1		1
869.664	Construction worker	REI	1			
119.267	Contract consultant	ESA	1	1	1	2
110.117	Corporate counsel	ESA	1			
168.167	Credit/collection manager	SIE		1		1
003.167	Development-and-planning engineer	IRE	2			
110.117	District attorney	ESA	2			
183.117	District manager	ESC	3			
132.067	Editor	ASI	7		2	2
166.267	Employment interviewer	SEC	1		1	1
020.167	Financial/investment analyst	IAS	4		1	1
050.067	Financial planner	IAS	1		1	1
373.364	Firefighter	RSE	2			
189.117	General manager	ESC	8	4	1	5
— —	Graduate student	—	19	3	3	6
045.107	Guidance counselor	SIA	2			

DOT	JOB TITLE	HOC	1960-1974	1975-1980		
				M	F	T
091.107	High-school-department chairperson	SAE	3			
091.107	High-school official	SAE	3		1	1
187.117	Hospital administrator	SEC			1	1
187.117	Hotel/restaurant manager	SEC	1			
012.167	Industrial engineer	ERI	1		1	1
250.257	Insurance agent/broker	ECS	6			
241.217	Insurance-claim adjuster	CSE	3		1	1
168.267	Insurance-claim examiner	SIE	3		1	1
169.167	Insurance underwriter	ESC	3			
166.167	Labor-relations consultant	SEC	1			
119.267	Law clerk	ESA	1		1	1
110.107	Law-school professor	ESA	2			
— —	Law student	—	4		2	2
110.107	Lawyer	ESA	32	1		1
100.127	Librarian	SAI	6		4	4
189.167	Management trainee	ESC	2			
163.117	Marketing manager	ESC	3			
050.067	Market-research analyst	IAS			1	1
078.261	Medical technologist	ISR	1			
152.041	Musician	ASI	1			
131.267	Newspaper reporter	ASI	4	1	1	2
169.167	Office manager	ESC	11		1	1
184.167	Operations manager	ESC	1			
195.167	Parole/probation officer	SIC	1			
166.117	Personnel manager	SEC	3			
143.062	Photographer	AIR	2			
196.263	Pilot/airplane	IRC	1			
375.263	Police officer	SRE		1		1
189.117	Private-business owner	ESC	8		1	1
163.267	Product-distribution manager	ESC	1			
189.117	Product manager	ESC.	2			
183.117	Production manager	ESC	1			
165.067	Public-relations practitioner	AES	8	1	1	2
045.107	Rehabilitation counselor	SIA	1			
290.477	Sales clerk	ESC	3			

DOT	JOB TITLE	HOC	1960-1974	1975-1980 M	F	T
163.167	Sales manager	ESC	8	1	1	2
279,357	Sales/service representative	ESC	9	2	1	3
600-800	Skilled trades	RIC	1	1		1
188.117	Social-welfare director	ESC	1		1	1
195.107	Social worker	SIC	7		1	1
070.101	Surgeon	ISA	1			
012.167	Systems analyst/electronic data processing	ERI	4			
160.167	Tax administrator	CES	1			
090.227	Teacher/college	SIA	24			
092.227	Teacher/elementary school	SAI	21	2	2	4
091.227	Teacher/high school	SAE	86	2	3	5
099.227	Teacher/other	SIR	16	1	4	5
094.227	Teacher/special education	SAI	1			
159.147	Television/radio personnel	AES	1			
184.117	Traffic analyst/manager	ESC	1		1	1
166.227	Training specialist	SEC	2			
252.157	Travel agent	ECS	1			
045.107	Vocational counselor	SIA	1			
131.067	Writer (fiction and nonfiction)	ASI	2			
131.267	Writer/technical	ASI	3	2		2
			457	40	52	92

Not to know what happened before one was born is to remain a child. — *Cicero*

HISTORY
GENERAL DESCRIPTION

History gives us a narrative account of the political, social, and cultural events and achievements that mankind has placed on record. Historians evaluate and analyze documents and record data relating to aspirations and deeds that past generations have left us, and use this knowledge to understand and interpret the present.

Historians frequently focus on an area that has special interest for them. Their specialties might embrace a period of time, an individual country, or the history of a field of human endeavor such as medicine, art, philosophy, feminism, military affairs.

In addition to being archivists and museum curators, historians can serve as consultants to publishers, TV, and movie producers, and they can do research for business and industrial firms, social and governmental agencies.

Students who major in history for their own educational development can use this training to enter a wide variety of occupations that suit their personalities and interests. The knowledge and training students gain in this major — together with additional skills they acquire through electives — have enabled many to find congenial employment in sales, brokerage and publishing houses, the media, insurance, and government. As they build up experience, graduates have frequently progressed to executive positions.

With a bachelor's degree, you can get entry jobs in government service, communications, banking, finance, and sales. You need an advanced degree to consider yourself a professional historian and to find jobs in research or archival work. Those who go on for additional training often become lawyers or college teachers.

CAREER LEADS

DOT	JOB TITLE	HOC
188.117	Administrative officer/government service	ESC
191.287	Appraiser/art	ESC
101.167	Archivist	SAI
188.117	Arts-and-Humanities-Council director	ESC
186.117	Bank officer	ESC
052.067	Biographer	SEI
100.387	Cataloger	SAI
090.117	College/university official	SIA
131.067	Columnist/commentator	ASI
131.087	Continuity writer	ASI
131.267	Correspondent	ASI
131.067	Critic (book, drama, film)	ASI
188.117	Cultural-affairs officer	ESC
168.267	Customs inspector	SIE
102.017	Curator (art galleries, museums)	AEI
090.161	Department head/college	SIA
090.167	Director of institutional research	SIA
052.167	Director/research (motion picture, radio, TV)	SEI
052.067	Director/state-historical society	SEI
132.067	Editor/news	ASI
132.067	Editor/publications	ASI
188.167	Election supervisor	ESC
055.067	Ethnologist	IAR
131.267	Foreign correspondent	ASI
188.117	Foreign-service officer	ESC
293.157	Fund raiser	ESC
052.067	Genealogist	SEI
052.067	Historian	SEI
052.067	Historian/dramatic arts	SEI
055.067	Historical archaeologist	IAR
250.257	Insurance agent/broker	ECS
059.267	Intelligence specialist	SIA
110.107	Lawyer	ESA
100.127	Librarian	SAI
189.167	Management trainee	ESC
187.117	Manager/chamber of commerce	SEC

DOT	JOB TITLE	HOC
132.267	Manuscript reader	ASI
131.067	Movie critic	ASI
102.381	Museum technician	AEI
131.267	Newscaster	ASI
131.267	News editor	ASI
119.267	Paralegal assistant	ESA
051.067	Political scientist	SIA
165.067	Public-relations practitioner	AEC
090.167	Registrar, college/university	SIA
259.357	Sales representative, radio/television time	ECS
131.087	Script reader	ASI
195.107	Social worker	SIC
102.117	Supervisor/historic sites	AEI
119.287	Title examiner	ESA
090.227	Teacher/college	SIA
091.227	Teacher/high school	SAE
353.167	Tour guide	SRE
252.157	Travel agent	ECS
131.067	Writer (prose, fiction, nonfiction)	ASI

HIRING INSTITUTIONS

Air, Bus, and Rail Lines
Archives
Banks, Savings/Commercial
Business Corporations
Chambers of Commerce
Colleges and Schools
Educational Institutions
Film Companies
Foundations, Non-Profit
Government Agencies
      Civil Rights Commission
      Consumer Affairs Office
      Education Department
      Environmental Protection Agency
      Federal Communications Agency
      Foreign Service Department
      Government Printing Office
      Health and Human Services Department
      International Trade Commission
      Justice Department
      Labor Department
      Library of Congress
      National Archives
      Social Security Administration
      Vista
Historical Societies
Industries, Manufacturing
Insurance Companies
Investment Firms
Libraries
Magazines and Newspapers
Museums
National and State Parks
Professional Periodicals
Public-Relations Firms
Publishing Companies
Radio/Television Stations
Social-Service Agencies
Travel Agencies

CURRENT OCCUPATIONS OF GRADUATES
WHO MAJORED IN HISTORY

DOT	JOB TITLE	HOC	1960-1974	1975-1980 M	F	T
160.167	Accountant	CES	5	2		2
160.167	Accounting manager	CES	2	1		1
188.117	Administrative officer/ government service	ESC	8			
164.117	Advertising manager	AES	2			
001.061	Architect	AIR		1		1
— —	Armed services	—	37	7		7
160.162	Auditor	CES	2	1		1
186.117	Bank officer	ESC	16	1		1
183.117	Branch manager	ESC	2			
161.117	Budget analyst	CES		1		1
189.117	Business executive	ESC	20	3		3
162.157	Buyer	ECS	2			
186.117	Cashier/bank	ESC	2			
120.007	Clergy member	SAI	4			
209.562	Clerk	CIE	4			
090.117	College/university official	SIA	11	1		1
213.362	Computer operator	CIS	1	1		1
213.132	Computer-operations supervisor	CIS	1			
020.187	Computer programer	IAS	7		1	1
169.664	Construction worker	REI		1	1	2
182.167	Contractor	ERI	1			
094.117	Coordinator of special services/education	SAI	6			
110.117	Corporate counsel	ESA	4			
160.167	Cost accountant	CES	1			
160.267	Cost estimator	CES	1			
191.267	Credit analyst	ESC	1	1		1
186.167	Credit-and-collection manager	SIE	2			
188.167	Customs officer	ESC	2			
— —	Dental student	—	1			
003.167	Development-and- planning engineer	IRE	1			
110.117	District attorney	ESA	2			
183.117	District manager	ESC	2			

DOT	JOB TITLE	HOC	1960-1974	1975-1980 M	F	T
050.067	Economist	IAS	1			
132.067	Editor	ASI	1			
092.137	Elementary-school official	SAI				
166.267	Employment interviewer	SEC	2			
186.167	Estate planner	ESC	5			
020.167	Financial/investment analyst	IAS	4			
050.067	Financial planner	IAS			1	1
373.364	Firefighter	RSE	2	1		1
189.117	General manager	ESC	15	1		1
— —	Graduate student	—	21	9	1	10
045.107	Guidance counselor	SIA	5		1	1
091.107	High-school-department chairperson	SAE	6			
091.107	High-school official	SAE	7			
187.117	Hospital administrator	SEC	5			
187.117	Hotel/restaurant manager	SEC	1			
012.167	Industrial engineer	ERI	2			
250.257	Insurance agent/broker	ECS	7	1		1
241.217	Insurance-claim adjuster	CSE	1	1		1
168.267	Insurance-claim examiner	SIE	7	1	2	3
169.167	Insurance underwriter	ESC	8	1		1
376.367	Investigator	SRE	2	1		1
111.107	Judge	ESA	1			
029.261	Laboratory technician	IRA	2			
119.267	Law clerk	ESA	4	3		3
— —	Law student	—	15	2	2	4
110.107	Lawyer	ESA	72	4	3	7
100.127	Librarian	SAI	5		2	2
189.167	Management trainee	ESC	3	3		3
163.117	Marketing manager	ESC	3	1		1
050.067	Market-research analyst	IAS	3			
078.261	Medical technologist	ISR	1			
131.267	Newspaper reporter	ASI	3			
169.167	Office manager	ESC	13			
184.167	Operations manager	ESC	1			
195.167	Parole/probation officer	SIC	4			

DOT	JOB TITLE	HOC	1960-1974	1975-1980		
				M	F	T
166.117	Personnel manager	SEC	5	1	1	2
143.062	Photographer	AIR	1			
070.101	Physician	ISA	1			
196.263	Pilot/airplane	IRC	1			
375.263	Police officer	SRE	5	5		5
189.117	Private-business owner	ESC	12	1		1
163.267	Product-distribution manager	ESC	2			
189.117	Product manager	ESC	3			
183.117	Production manager	ESC	3			
045.107	Psychologist	SIA	4			
165.067	Public-relations practitioner	AES		1		1
070.101	Radiologist	ISA	1			
250.357	Real-estate agent/broker	ECS		1		1
045.107	Rehabilitation counselor	SIA	1			
189.117	Research-and-development director	ESC	1		1	1
160.167	Revenue agent	CES	7	1		1
290.477	Sales clerk	ESC	1		1	1
163.167	Sales manager	ESC	5			
279.357	Sales/service representative	ESC	23	5		5
186.167	Securities trader	ESC	3			
189.167	Security officer	ESC	1	1		1
— —	Seminarian	—	2	1		1
600-800	Skilled trades	RIC	6	2		2
188.117	Social-welfare director	ESC	2			
195.107	Social worker	SIC	7	1		1
375.167	Special agent/FBI	SRE	1			
251.157	Stock broker	ECS	2			
185.167	Store manager	ESI	4	1		1
012.167	Systems analyst/electronic data processing	ERI	2			
003.167	Systems engineer	IRE	1			
090.227	Teacher/college	SIA	13			
092.227	Teacher/elementary school	SAI	30	5	3	8
091.227	Teacher/high school	SAE	72	7	2	9

DOT	JOB TITLE	HOC	1960-1974	1975-1980 M	F	T
099.227	Teacher/other	SIR	21	1		1
094.227	Teacher/special education	SAI	1			
184.117	Traffic analyst/manager	ESC	2	1		1
166.227	Training specialist	SEC	5			
184.117	Transportation manager	ESC	1	1		1
199.167	Urban planner	ICR	1			
			637	86	22	108

Let your advance worrying become advance thinking and planning. — *Sir Winston Churchill*

MANAGEMENT
GENERAL DESCRIPTION

B usiness managers plan, organize, staff, and direct a business or institution. They may run an entire organization or one of its units.

They become involved in such areas as managing human resources, labor relations, resolving conflicts, motivating and evaluating subordinates, negotiating and decision-making. A variety of fast-paced, action-oriented activities make effective writing and speaking skills a must for business managers — on the phone, in staff meetings, or at large conferences.

Managers need flexibility to play different roles at different times: institutional symbol, spokesperson, negotiator. As employees advance in any kind of organizational structure —manufacturer, hospital, financial institution, college, or consulting firm — they can expect to take on managerial responsibilities that call for increasingly-specialized knowledge and skills.

Places of employment usually include firms which manufacture products such as machinery, food and clothing, or those that provide services, such as airlines and telephone companies. You can improve your chances of advancing in your job if you develop proficiency in data-processing and statistics. And if you train yourself to write clearly and to speak effectively, you will have the tools that most executives say you need to succeed in business.

The bachelor's degree in management, with electives in communications and the new technologies, opens up a wide variety of beginning jobs in business, industry, and government. Additional education such as an MBA, in the same or a related field, is helpful and often essential as you take on greater managerial responsibilities.

CAREER LEADS

DOT	JOB TITLE	HOC
160.167	Accountant (budget, cost, systems)	CES
164.167	Account executive	AES
020.167	Actuary	IAS
188.117	Administrative officer/government service	ESC
164.117	Advertising manager	AES
193.162	Air-traffic controller	RIE
160.162	Auditor	CES
186.117	Bank officer	ESC
162.157	Broker's floor representative	ECS
160.207	Budget consultant	CES
161.117	Budget officer	CES
160.167	Bursar	CES
186.117	Business manager/education	ESC
241.217	Claim adjustor	CSE
191.167	Claim agent	ESC
241.267	Claim examiner	CSE
161.267	Clerical-methods analyst	CES
213.132	Computer-operations supervisor	CIS
020.187	Computer programer	IAS
169.207	Conciliator	ESC
096.121	Consumer-service consultant	SRI
119.267	Contract consultant	ESA
186.117	Controller	ESC
191.267	Credit analyst	ESC
168.167	Credit-and-collection manager	SIE
166.117	Director/industrial relations	SEC
189.117	Director/research and development	ESC
166.267	Employment interviewer	SEC
132.037	Editor/trade journal	ASI
012.167	Efficiency expert	ERI
169.267	Financial-aid counselor	ESC
020.167	Financial analyst	IAS
161.267	Forms analyst	CES
187.117	Hospital administrator	SEC
184.117	Import-export agent	ESC
012.167	Industrial engineer	ERI
109.067	Information scientist	IRC

DOT	JOB TITLE	HOC
250.257	Insurance agent/broker	ECS
168.267	Internal-revenue investigator	SIE
166.267	Job analyst	SEC
166.167	Labor-relations representative	SEC
110.107	Lawyer	ESA
186.267	Loan officer	ESC
161.117	Management analyst	CES
189.167	Management trainee	ESC
187.167	Manager/casino	SEC
187.117	Manager/chamber of commerce	SEC
163.117	Manager/contracts	ESC
186.117	Manager/financial institution	ESC
163.117	Manager/promotion	ESC
185.167	Manager/retail store	ESI
050.067	Market-research analyst	IAS
169.167	Office manager	ESC
184.117	Operations manager	ESC
166.117	Personnel manager	SEC
166.167	Placement director	SEC
189.117	Product manager	ESC
183.117	Production manager	ESC
163.167	Property-disposal officer	ESC
162.157	Purchasing agent	ECS
197.167	Purser	REI
250.357	Real-estate agent/broker	ECS
160.167	Revenue agent	CES
161.267	Reports analyst	CES
168.264	Safety inspector	SIE
251.257	Sales agent/financial services	ECS
186.167	Securities trader	ESC
357.167	Special agent/FBI	SRE
251.157	Stock broker	ECS
012.167	Systems analyst	ERI
090.227	Teacher/college	SIA
119.287	Title examiner	ESA
184.167	Traffic manager	ESC
166.227	Training instructor	SEC
186.117	Trust officer/bank	ESC

DOT	JOB TITLE	HOC
166.167	Wage-and-salary administrator	SEC
131.267	Writer/technical publications	ASI

HIRING INSTITUTIONS

Accounting Firms
Advertising Departments and Agencies
Air, Bus, and Rail Lines
Banks, Savings/Commercial
Brokerage Houses
Business Corporations
Civic and Taxpayers' Associations
Colleges and Schools
Department Stores
Educational Institutions
Engineering Firms
Foundations, Non-Profit
Government Agencies
      Civil Service Commission
      Consumer Affairs Office
      Energy Department
      General Accounting Office
      International Trade Commission
      Labor Department
      Management and Budget Office
      Securities and Exchange Commission
      Social Security Administration
      Vista
Hospitals
Industries, Manufacturing
Insurance Companies
Investment Firms
Magazines, Newspapers
Management-Consulting Firms
Manufacturing and Processing Firms
Market Research Departments and Firms

Nursing Homes
Personnel Departments
Professional Journals
Publishing Companies
Radio/Television Stations
Regional-Planning Councils and Associations
Research-and-Development Firms
Trade Associations
Utility Companies

CURRENT OCCUPATIONS OF GRADUATES WHO MAJORED IN MANAGEMENT

DOT	JOB TITLE	HOC	1960-1974	1975-1980 M	F	T
160.167	Accountant	CES	16	18	2	20
160.167	Accounting manager	CES	6	2	3	5
160.167	Accounting partner	CES	1			
020.167	Actuary	IAS	1			
188.117	Administrative officer/ government service	ESC	19	3	2	5
164.117	Advertising manager	AES	4	1		1
— —	Armed services	—	17	8		8
099.167	Audiovisual specialist	SIE	1			
160.162	Auditor	CES	11	4		4
186.117	Bank officer	ESC	46	19	5	24
183.117	Branch manager	ESC	10	3		3
161.117	Budget analyst	CES	5	4	2	6
189.117	Business executive	ESC	52	12	5	17
162.157	Buyer	ECS	6	3	2	5
186.117	Cashier/bank	ESC	2	3	2	5
022.061	Chemist/research	IAR	1			
079.101	Chiropractor	SIR	1			
110.117	Claim attorney	ESA			1	1
120.007	Clergy member	SAI	3			
209.562	Clerk	CIE	12	12	7	19
090.117	College/university official	SIA	2	1		1
213.362	Computer operator	CIS	2		2	2
213.132	Computer-operations supervisor	CIS	4	8		8

DOT	JOB TITLE	HOC	1960-1974	1975-1980		
				M	F	T
020.187	Computer programer	IAS	21	24	2	26
869.664	Construction worker	REI	1	2		2
119.267	Contract consultant	ESA	1			
094.117	Coordinator of special services/education	SAI	1			
160.167	Cost accountant	CES	8	1		1
160.267	Cost estimator	CES	1	2		2
191.267	Credit analyst	ESC	2	3	1	4
168.167	Credit-and-collection manager	SIE	5	3	2	5
188.167	Customs officer	ESC	1	1		1
003.167	Development-and-planning engineer	IRE	4	2		2
183.117	District manager	ESC	7	3		3
050.067	Economist	IAS	1			
050.067	Economist/price	IAS		1		1
132.067	Editor	ASI	1			
003.061	Electrical engineer	IRE	4	2		2
092.137	Elementary-school official	SAI	1			
166.267	Employment interviewer	SEC	2			
020.167	Financial/investment analyst	IAS	3	1		1
050.067	Financial planner	IAS	5	2	3	5
373.364	Firefighter	RSE	2	2		2
187.167	Funeral director	SEC		1	1	2
189.117	General manager	ESC	45	37	5	42
— —	Graduate student	—	5	1	1	2
045.107	Guidance counselor	SIA	2			
091.107	High-school-department chairperson	SAE	1			
091.107	High-school official	SAE	2			
187.117	Hospital administrator	SEC	1	1	2	3
012.167	Industrial engineer	ERI	9	2	2	4
250.257	Insurance agent/broker	ECS	16	6		6
241.217	Insurance-claim adjuster	CSE	4	5		5
168.267	Insurance-claim examiner	SIE	6	2	2	4
241.217	Insurance-claim investigator	CSE	2	1		1

DOT	JOB TITLE	HOC	1960-1974	1975-1980 M	F	T
186.117	Insurance-and-risk manager	ESC	1	1		1
169.167	Insurance underwriter	ESC	14	1		1
142.051	Interior designer/decorator	AIS	1			
376.367	Investigator	SRE	3	1		1
111.107	Judge	ESA	1			
029.261	Laboratory technician	IRA		1		1
166.167	Labor-relations consultant	SEC	1		1	1
119.267	Law clerk	ESA	2	1		1
— —	Law student	—		3		3
110.107	Lawyer	ESA	6		1	1
100.127	Librarian	SAI			1	1
230.367	Mail carrier	CSR	2		1	1
012.167	Management/methods engineer	ERI	6			
189.167	Management trainee	ESC	4	11	5	16
163.117	Marketing manager	ESC	9	2		2
050.067	Market-research analyst	IAS	11		1	1
— —	Medical student	—		1		1
152.041	Musician	ASI	1			
169.167	Office manager	ESC	42	7	2	9
184.167	Operations manager	ESC	7	15		15
079.101	Optometrist	SIR		1		1
195.167	Parole/probation officer	SIC	2			
166.117	Personnel manager	SEC	16	9	4	13
196.263	Pilot/airplane	IRC	2			
375.263	Police officer	SRE	4	7		7
189.117	Private-business owner	ESC	13	1		1
163.267	Product-distribution manager	ESC	1			
189.117	Product manager	ESC	14	8	1	9
183.117	Production manager	ESC	14	7	1	8
165.067	Public-relations practitioner	AES	5	3		3
162.157	Purchasing agent	ECS	12	1	1	2
012.167	Quality-control engineer	ERI	1	1		1
070.101	Radiologist	ISA	1			
250.357	Real-estate agent/broker	ECS	4	1	2	3

DOT	JOB TITLE	HOC	1960-1974	1975-1980		
				M	F	T
045.107	Rehabilitation counselor	SIA	1			
189.117	Research-and-development director	ESC	5		1	1
160.167	Revenue agent	CES	3			
290.477	Sales clerk	ESC	14	5	1	6
163.167	Sales manager	ESC	24	5		5
279.357	Sales/service representative	ESC	36	19	3	22
020.167	Securities analyst	IAS		2		2
186.167	Securities trader	ESC	2	1		1
186.167	Security officer	ESC		1		1
600-800	Skilled trades	RIC	10	10		10
195.107	Social worker	SIC	3	2		2
054.067	Sociologist	SIA		1		1
375.167	Special agent/FBI	SRE	2			
020.067	Statistician	IAS	1			
251.157	Stock broker	ECS	2	5		5
185.167	Store manager	ESI		5		5
070.101	Surgeon	ISA	1			
012.167	Systems analyst/electronic data processing	ERI	23	2		2
003.167	Systems engineer	IRE	3			
160.167	Tax administrator	CES			1	1
090.227	Teacher/college	SIA	3	1		1
092.227	Teacher/elementary school	SAI	3			
091.227	Teacher/high school	SAE	17	2	3	5
099.227	Teacher/other	SIR	4	1	2	3
184.117	Traffic analyst/manager	ESC	5	3		3
137.267	Translator	ASI	1			
184.117	Transportation manager	ESC	4	2		2
186.117	Trust officer/bank	ESC	4			
			757	356	86	442

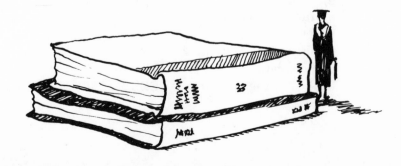

Invention is the mother of necessity.
— *Thorstein Veblen*

MARKETING
GENERAL DESCRIPTION

Marketing seeks to satisfy the needs and wants of consumers by exchanging goods for money or credit. Marketing also aims to use efficiently an economy's assets and productive capacity.

Managers in charge of marketing develop practices to control the flow of goods from production-stage to point-of-purchase. They find ways to anticipate and stimulate demand for a product or service. Their activities include advertising, marketing research, brand management, international distribution, and transportation. In marketing, they analyze the opinions and tastes of the buying public, the means of disseminating information — radio, TV, magazines, direct mail — and the most efficient, economical ways to get products to the marketplace and to the consumer.

Since the marketing manager's activities touch on so many aspects of a business enterprise, you can improve your prospects in this field with courses in economics, sociology, psychology, political science, statistics — and especially in speech and writing.

Employers include large business and industrial firms but also smaller companies, private research organizations, and advertising agencies. Retail and wholesale trade, insurance, travel, and real estate are other areas where your training can open up job opportunities.

While the bachelor's degree qualifies you for a broad range of beginning jobs, you will probably need a master's degree for more responsible positions.

CAREER LEADS

DOT	JOB TITLE	HOC
160.167	Accountant (budget, cost, systems)	CES
164.167	Account executive	AES
020.167	Actuary	IAS
188.117	Administrative officer/government service	ESC
164.117	Advertising manager	AES
188.167	Appraiser	ESC
191.117	Artist's manager	ESC
186.117	Bank officer	ESC
191.117	Booking agent	ESC
160.207	Budget consultant	CES
186.117	Business manager/education	ESC
241.217	Claim adjustor	CSE
191.167	Claim agent	ESC
241.267	Claim examiner	CSE
213.132	Computer-operations supervisor	CIS
020.186	Computer programer	IAS
169.207	Conciliator	ESC
188.117	Consumer affairs/director	ESC
096.121	Consumer-service consultant	SRI
094.117	Coordinator of special services/education	SAI
191.267	Credit analyst	ESC
168.167	Credit-and-collection manager	SIE
166.117	Director/industrial relations	SEC
189.117	Director/research and development	ESC
166.267	Employment interviewer	SEC
132.037	Editor/trade journal	ASI
169.267	Financial-aid counselor	ESC
020.167	Financial analyst	IAS
166.267	Hospital-insurance representative	SEC
184.117	Import-export agent	ESC
187.117	Hotel/restaurant manager	SEC
012.167	Industrial engineer	ERI
109.067	Information scientist	IRC
250.257	Insurance agent/broker	ECS
168.267	Internal-revenue investigator	SIE
166.167	Labor-relations representative	SEC
110.107	Lawyer	ESA

DOT	JOB TITLE	HOC
191.117	Literary agent	ESC
189.167	Management trainee	ESC
187.117	Manager/chamber of commerce	SEC
186.117	Manager/financial institution	ESC
184.167	Manager/flight reservations	ESC
163.117	Manager/promotion	ESC
185.167	Manager/retail store	ESI
050.067	Market-research analyst	IAS
169.167	Office manager	ESC
184.117	Operations manager	ESC
166.117	Personnel manager	SEC
262.157	Pharmaceutical detailer	ESR
166.167	Placement director	SEC
189.117	Product manager	ESC
183.117	Production manager	ESC
163.167	Property-disposal officer	ESC
165.067	Public-relations representative	AES
162.157	Purchasing agent	ECS
197.167	Purser	REI
250.357	Real-estate agent/broker	ECS
161.267	Reports analyst	CES
160.167	Revenue agent	CES
251.257	Sales agent/financial services	ECS
251.257	Sales agent/psychological tests	ECS
163.167	Sales manager	ESC
275.257	Sales representative (computers and electronic data processing systems)	ESI
186.167	Securities trader	ESC
020.167	Statistician	IAS
251.157	Stock broker	ECS
012.167	Systems analyst	ERI
090.227	Teacher/college	SIA
184.167	Traffic manager	ESC
166.227	Training instructor	SEC
186.117	Trust officer/bank	ESC
199.167	Urban planner	ICR
131.267	Writer/technical publications	ASI

HIRING INSTITUTIONS

Accounting Firms
Advertising Departments and Agencies
Air, Bus, and Rail Lines
Banks, Savings/Commercial
Brokerage Houses
Business Corporations
Chambers of Commerce
Civic and Taxpayers' Associations
Colleges and Schools
Consumer Organizations
Department Stores
Educational Institutions
Employment Agencies
Film Companies
Foundations, Non-Profit
Fund-Raising Firms
Government Agencies
      Consumer Affairs Office
      International Trade Commission
      Securities and Exchange Commission
      Social Security Administration
Import/Export Companies
Industries, Manufacturing
Insurance Companies
Investment Firms
Labor Unions
Magazines, Newspapers
Manufacturing and Processing Firms
Market Research Departments and Firms
Personnel Departments
Pharmaceutical Companies
Professional Journals
Public-Relations Firms
Publishing Companies
Radio/Television Stations
Research-and-Development Firms
Trade Associations
Travel Agencies
Utility Companies

CURRENT OCCUPATIONS OF GRADUATES
WHO MAJORED IN MARKETING

DOT	JOB TITLE	HOC	1960-1974	1975-1980 M	F	T
160.167	Accountant	CES	11	3	2	5
160.167	Accounting manager	CES	2	1	1	2
150.047	Actor	ASE	1			
020.167	Actuary	IAS			1	1
188.117	Administrative officer/ government service	ESC	21	1	1	2
164.117	Advertising manager	AES	2	1		1
070.101	Anesthesiologist	ISA			1	1
— —	Armed services	—	18			
144.061	Artist	AIR		1		1
160.162	Auditor	CES	5	1		1
186.117	Bank officer	ESC	24	3	1	4
183.117	Branch manager	ESC	4			
161.117	Budget analyst	CES	6			
189.117	Business executive	ESC	45	7	2	9
162.157	Buyer	ECS	10	1	2	3
186.117	Cashier, bank	ESC	4	1		1
209.562	Clerk	CIE	6	11	3	14
090.117	College/university official	SIA	2			
213.363	Computer operator	CIS	4	5	1	6
213.132	Computer-operations supervisor	CIS	1			
020.187	Computer programer	IAS	7	10	1	11
869.664	Construction worker	REI	2			
094.117	Coordinator of special services/education	SAI	3			
160.167	Cost accountant	CES	2			
191.267	Credit analyst	ESC	2	1		1
168.167	Credit-and-collection manager	SIE	4	2		2
003.167	Development-and-planning engineer	IRE	3			
183.117	District manager	ESC	9	1		1
050.067	Economist	IAS	2		1	1
050.067	Economist/price	IAS	1			
132.067	Editor	ASI	1		1	1
166.267	Employment interviewer	SEC			1	1

DOT	JOB TITLE	HOC	1960-1974	1975-1980 M	F	T
020.167	Financial/investment analyst	IAS	8	1		1
050.067	Financial planner	IAS	1		1	1
373.364	Firefighter	RSE	1			
187.167	Funeral director	SEC	1			
189.117	General manager	ESC	24	2	2	4
— —	Graduate student	—	3	1		1
045.107	Guidance counselor	SIA	2			
091.107	High-school-department chairperson	SAE	1			
091.107	High school official	SAE	1			
187.117	Hotel/restaurant manager	SEC		1		1
012.167	Industrial engineer	ERI	2	2		2
250.257	Insurance agent/broker	ECS	8	1	2	3
241.217	Insurance-claim adjuster	CSE	1	2		2
168.267	Insurance-claim examiner	SIE	6			
241.217	Insurance-claim investigator	CSE	1			
169.167	Insurance underwriter	ESC	4	1		1
119.267	Law clerk	ESA		1		1
— —	Law student	—	2	1		1
110.107	Lawyer	ESA	15			
100.127	Librarian	SAI		2		2
230.367	Mail carrier	CSR	1	1		1
012.167	Management/methods engineer	ERI	2			
189.167	Management trainee	ESC	6	2		2
163.117	Marketing manager	ESC	7	3	1	4
050.067	Market-research analyst	IAS	9	4	2	6
169.167	Office manager	ESC	12	3	1	4
184.167	Operations manager	ESC	5	3		3
166.117	Personnel manager	SEC	11	2	2	4
070.101	Physician	ISA	1			
196.263	Pilot/airplane	IRC	1			
375.263	Police officer	SRE	2	1		1
189.117	Private-business owner	ESC	10	2		2
163.267	Product-distribution manager	ESC	4			

DOT	JOB TITLE	HOC	1960-1974	1975-1980 M	F	T
189.117	Product manager	ESC	9	1	3	4
183.117	Production manager	ESC	4	2		2
045.107	Psychologist	SIA		1		1
165.067	Public-relations practitioner	AES	4		1	1
162.157	Purchasing agent	ECS	3	3		3
012.167	Quality-control engineer	ERI		1		1
250.357	Real-estate agent/broker	ECS	2	1		1
189.117	Research-and-development director	ESC	5			
160.167	Revenue agent	CES	1			
290.477	Sales clerk	ESC	20	6		6
163.167	Sales manager	ESC	27	11	1	12
279.357	Sales/service representative	ESC	41	10	3	13
020.167	Securities analyst	IAS	2			
186.167	Securities trader	ESC	1			
— —	Seminarian	—	1			
600-800	Skilled trades	RIC	7	1		1
195.107	Social worker	SIC	3		1	1
020.167	Statistician	IAS		1		1
251.157	Stock broker	ECS	5			
185.167	Store manager	ESI	3	1	1	2
012.167	Systems analyst/electronic data processing	ERI	9	1		1
160.162	Tax accountant	CES	1			
090.227	Teacher/college	SIA	1			
092.227	Teacher/elementary school	SAI	2	1	1	2
091.227	Teacher/high school	SAE	17	1		1
099.227	Teacher/other	SIR	4		1	1
094.227	Teacher/special education	SAI		1		1
184.117	Traffic analyst/manager	ESC	1	2	1	3
166.227	Training specialist	SEC	1			
184.117	Transportation manager	ESC	1	1		1
186.117	Trust officer/bank	ESC	1		1	1
199.167	Urban planner	ICR	1			
131.267	Writer/technical	ASI	1			
			532	**132**	**44**	**176**

Difficulties strengthen the mind, as labor does the body. —*Seneca*

MATHEMATICS AND COMPUTER SCIENCE
GENERAL DESCRIPTION

Mathematicians study concepts and theories to help them solve problems that involve quantitative relationships. Those who do research to discover new theories or to increase basic knowledge call themselves *theoretical* mathematicians. Those who develop techniques and approaches to solve problems in the physical and social sciences, or in business and industry, refer to themselves as *applied* mathematicians.

Computer scientists learn how to structure and operate computer systems and they study the principles that underlie their design and programing. Students work with circuitry, logic, programing languages, file structures, and systems architectures. As computer scientists, they also explore new areas of intellectual activity where computers can come creatively into play.

Although for a while opportunities in colleges and universities had dwindled for mathematicians as a result of shrinking enrollments, math graduates still found employment as statisticians, economists, systems analysts, and life scientists by taking a minor in one of these subjects while in college.

Computer-science graduates generally find jobs as programers and systems analysts, with many specialties in each area. A background in accounting, management, or economics may qualify you for work in the business sector; for jobs in scientifically-oriented establishments you can improve your prospects by getting some training in the physical sciences, mathematics, or engineering.

In many colleges, computer science has developed as part of the Mathematics Department, but there is a growing tendency for these two disciplines to become independent departments.

CAREER LEADS

DOT	JOB TITLE	HOC
160.167	Accountant (budget, cost, systems)	CES
020.167	Actuary	IAS
196.167	Airplane navigator	IRC
196.263	Airplane pilot	IRC
193.162	Air-traffic controller	RIE
001.061	Architect	AIR
161.117	Budget officer	CES
160.167	Bursar/education	CES
018.261	Cartographer	RCI
020.062	Computer-applications engineer	IAS
020.187	Computer programer	IAS
003.167	Computer-systems engineer	IRE
020.067	Computing analyst	IAS
199.267	Cryptanalyst	ICR
102.017	Curator (art galleries, museums)	AEI
169.167	Data-processing manager	ESC
020.162	Data-reduction analyst	IAS
020.167	Demographer	IAS
090.167	Department head/college	SIA
090.167	Director of institutional research	SIA
188.167	Director of vital statistics	ESC
017.261	Draftsman	RIA
012.167	Efficiency expert	ERI
020.067	Engineering analyst	IAS
001.061	Environmental planner	AIR
186.167	Estate planner	ESC
020.167	Financial analyst	IAS
293.157	Fund raiser	ESC
018.167	Geodetic computer	RCI
109.067	Information scientist	IRC
250.257	Insurance agent/broker	ECS
168.267	Internal-revenue investigator	SIE
110.107	Lawyer	ESA
189.167	Management trainee	ESC
050.067	Market-research analyst	IAS
020.162	Mathematical technician	IAS
020.067	Mathematician (applied, research)	IAS

DOT	JOB TITLE	HOC
025.062	Meteorologist	IRA
020.067	Operations-research analyst	IAS
099.117	Principal/education	SIE
162.157	Purchasing agent	ECS
012.167	Quality-control supervisor	ERI
275.257	Sales representative (computer and electronic data processing systems)	ESI
186.167	Securities trader/banking	ESC
020.167	Statistician/applied	IAS
020.067	Statistician/mathematical	IAS
251.157	Stockbroker	ECS
002.061	Stress analyst	IRE
012.167	Systems analyst	ERI
020.067	Systems analyst/engineering-scientific	IAS
090.227	Teacher/college	SIA
017.281	Technical illustrator	RIA

HIRING INSTITUTIONS

Banks, Savings/Commercial
Business Corporations
Colleges and Schools
Educational Institutions
Engineering Firms
Government Agencies
      Agriculture Department
      Airports
      Civil Service Commission
      Consumer Affairs Commission
      Defense Department
      Energy Department
      Federal Communications Commission
      General Accounting Office
      Internal Revenue Service
      Management and Budget Office
      National Science Foundation
      Nuclear Regulation Commission

Securities and Exchange Commission
Social Security Administration
Treasury Department
Industries, Manufacturing
Insurance Companies
Investment Firms
Market-Research Departments and Firms
Professional/Technical Journals
Publishing Companies
Research-and-Development Firms
Test-Development Corporations
Utility Companies
Weather Bureaus and Companies

CURRENT OCCUPATIONS OF GRADUATES WHO MAJORED IN MATHEMATICS/COMPUTER SCIENCE

DOT	JOB TITLE	HOC	1960-1974	1975-1980 M	F	T
160.167	Accountant	CES	2			
160.167	Accounting manager	CES	3			
020.167	Actuary	IAS	8	1	1	2
188.117	Administrative officer/ government service	ESC	3			
— —	Armed services	—	12			
160.162	Auditor	CES	1	1		1
186.117	Bank officer	ESC	8			
183.117	Branch manager	ESC	1			
161.117	Budget analyst	CES	1	1		1
189.117	Business executive	ESC	15	1	1	2
022.161	Chemist	IAR		1		1
022.061	Chemist research	IAR	1			
120.007	Clergy member	SAI	1			
209.562	Clerk	CIE	2	2	1	3
090.117	College/university official	SIA	1		1	1
213.362	Computer operator	CIS	1	3		3
213.132	Computer-operations supervisor	CIS	10	1	3	4
020.187	Computer programer	IAS	45	17	9	26
119.267	Contract consultant	ESA	1			

DOT	JOB TITLE	HOC	1960-1974	1975-1980 M	F	T
160.167	Cost accountant	CES	1			
160.267	Cost estimator	CES			1	1
168.167	Credit-and-collection manager	SIE	3			
188.167	Customs officer	ESC	1			
003.167	Data-processing engineer	IRE	1	1		1
003.167	Development-and-planning engineer	IRE	6	1	1	2
183.117	District manager	ESC	3			
050.067	Economist	IAS	1			
003.061	Electrical engineer	IRE	2		1	1
092.137	Elementary-school official	SAI	1			
020.167	Financial/investment analyst	IAS	3			
050.067	Financial planner	IAS			1	1
189.117	General manager	ESC	13	1		1
— —	Graduate student	—	11	1	2	3
045.107	Guidance counselor	SIA	2			
091.107	High-school-department chairperson	SAE	2			
091.107	High-school official	SAE	3			
250.257	Insurance agent/broker	ECS	5			
168.267	Insurance-claim examiner	SIE	1			
186.117	Insurance-and-risk manager	ESC	1	1		1
169.167	Insurance underwriter	ESC	3			
029.261	Laboratory technician	IRA		1		1
— —	Law student	—	1		2	2
110.107	Lawyer	ESA	5			
100.127	Librarian	SAI	1			
012.167	Management/methods engineer	ERI	2	1		1
189.167	Management trainee	ESC	2			
163.117	Marketing manager	ESC	3			
050.067	Market-research analyst	IAS	5			
020.067	Mathematician	IAS	3	1	1	2
— —	Medical student	—	1			
169.167	Office manager	ESC	8	1		1

DOT	JOB TITLE	HOC	1960-1974	1975-1980		
				M	F	T
184.167	Operations manager	ESC	4	1		1
166.117	Personnel manager	SEC	5			
196.263	Pilot/airplane	IRC		1		1
375.263	Police officer	SRE	1			
189.117	Private-business owner	ESC	3			
189.117	Product manager	ESC	2			
165.067	Public-relations practitioner	AES	1			
189.117	Research-and-development director	ESC	2			
290.477	Sales clerk	ESC	2			
163.167	Sales manager	ESC	1			
279.357	Sales/service representative	ESC	4			
600-800	Skilled trades	RIC	8			
195.107	Social worker	SIC	4			
020.067	Statistician	IAS	1			
251.157	Stockbroker	ECS	1			
185.167	Store manager	ESI	2	1		1
012.167	Systems analyst/ electronic data processing	ERI	32	1		1
003.167	Systems engineer	IRE	1			
090.227	Teacher/college	SIA	20			
092.227	Teacher/elementary school	SAI	5	1		1
091.227	Teacher/high school	SAE	61	4	6	10
099.227	Teacher/other	SIR	13		2	2
094.227	Teacher/special education	SAI	1			
166.227	Training specialist	SEC	1			
186.117	Trust officer/bank	ESC	1			
			386	46	33	79

*When you travel, remember that a foreign country is
not designed to make you comfortable. It is
designed to make its own people comfortable.*
— *Clifton Fadiman*

MODERN LANGUAGES
GENERAL DESCRIPTION

L anguage is the system people use to express the ideas
and feelings they share as human beings. Through that
process, studying a language gives us a way to
understand the range of experience a particular culture has
enjoyed.

Jobs that require a foreign language as a primary skill
can be somewhat limited in number. Such jobs include teaching in schools and colleges, interpreting at the United Nations
or in foreign service, or broadcasting for radio and cable TV stations that transmit programs in Spanish, Italian, Japanese, and
other languages.

Language-study helps you to think quickly and logically,
to use words effectively, and to sharpen your memory. You can
apply this kind of training to electives in business, finance, or
other subjects you like, to round out further your preparation
for a career. You can improve your job prospects by finding
firms that will consider your language training an asset: multi-
national corporations with offices all over the world that deal in
oil, electronics, automobiles, and heavy machinery, and companies that export such products as tires, food, tools, hardware,
and other basic commodities.

Fields where you can apply your language training
include also travel and tourism, hotel service (there are 150
multilingual hotels in the United States), English newspapers
and magazines with foreign departments or editions
(*Reader's Digest* has 26 foreign-language editions), motion pictures, libraries, museums, and publishing companies.

Those who wish to become college instructors or professional linguists will need advanced training beyond the bachelor's degree.

CAREER LEADS

DOT	JOB TITLE	HOC
159.147	Announcer (radio and TV)	AES
055.067	Anthropological linguist	IAR
191.287	Appraiser/art	ESC
188.117	Arts-and-Humanities-Council director	ESC
099.167	Audiovisual specialist	SIE
052.067	Biographer	SEI
131.067	Book critic	ASI
100.387	Cataloger	SAI
090.117	College/university official	SIA
195.167	Community-organization worker	SIC
020.187	Computer programer	IAS
131.067	Copy writer/advertising	ASI
139.087	Crossword-puzzle maker	ASI
168.267	Customs inspector	SIE
090.167	Department head/college	SIA
132.067	Editor/greeting cards	ASI
166.267	Employment interviewer	SEC
059.067	Etymologist	SIA
352.367	Flight attendant	ESA
184.167	Flight-reservations manager	ESC
188.117	Foreign-service officer	ESC
090.107	Foreign-student advisor	SIA
165.117	Fund-raising director	AES
168.167	Immigration inspector	SIE
184.117	Import-export agent	ESC
059.267	Intelligence specialist	SIA
051.067	International-relations specialist	SIA
137.267	Interpreter	ASI
110.107	Lawyer	ESA
100.127	Librarian	SAI
189.167	Management trainee	ESC
132.267	Manuscript reader (print and publications)	ASI
102.381	Museum technician	AEI
131.267	Newswriter/foreign languages	ASI
059.067	Philologist	SIA
070.101	Physician	ISA

DOT	JOB TITLE	HOC
165.067	Public-relations representative	AES
109.267	Research assistant	IRC
059.067	Scientific linguist	SIA
195.107	Social worker	SIC
375.167	Special agent/FBI	SRE
090.227	Teacher/college	SIA
091.227	Teacher/high school	SAE
353.167	Tour guide	SRE
166.227	Training instructor	SEC
137.267	Translator	ASI
252.157	Travel agent	ECS
131.067	Writer (prose, fiction and nonfiction)	ASI
131.267	Writer/technical publications	ASI

HIRING INSTITUTIONS

Advertising Departments and Agencies
Air, Bus, and Rail Lines
Banks, Savings/Commercial
Bookstores
Business Corporations
Colleges and Schools
Department Stores
Film Companies
Fund-Raising Firms
Government Agencies
        Agency for International Development
        Airports
        Civil Rights Commission
        Civil Service Commission
        Commerce Department
        Consumer Affairs Office
        Educational Department
        Federal Communications Commission
        Federal Trade Commission
        Foreign Service Department
        Government Printing Office

    Immigration and Naturalization Service
    International Trade Commission
    Library of Congress
    National Archives
    National Foundation on the Arts and
      the Humanities
    Peace Corps
    Vista
Hotel Chains
Import/Export Companies
Industries, Manufacturing
Investment Firms
Labor Unions
Libraries
Literary Periodicals
Magazines, Newspapers
Museums
Professional Periodicals
Public-Relations Firms
Publishing Companies
Radio/Television Stations
Social-Service Agencies
Technical-Writing Services
Travel Agencies
United Nations

CURRENT OCCUPATIONS OF GRADUATES
WHO MAJORED IN MODERN LANGUAGES

DOT	JOB TITLE	HOC	1960-1974	1975-1980 M	F	T
160.167	Accounting manager	CES	1			
150.047	Actor	ASE	1			
188.117	Administrative officer/ government service	ESC	3			
— —	Armed services	—	5	1		1
186.117	Bank officer	ESC	4	1	1	2
161.117	Budget analyst	CES	1			
189.117	Business executive	ESC	4		1	1
162.157	Buyer	ECS	1			
079.101	Chiropractor	SIR	1			
120.007	Clergy member	SAI	2	1		1
209.562	Clerk	CIE			5	5
090.167	College-department head	SIA	1	1		1
090.117	College/university official	SIA	3			
119.267	Contract consultant	ESA			1	1
131.067	Copy writer	ASI	1			
188.167	Customs officer	ESC	1			
132.067	Editor	ASI	2			
189.117	General manager	ESC	1		1	1
— —	Graduate student	—	4		1	1
045.107	Guidance counselor	SIA			1	1
091.107	High-school official	SAE	1			
187.117	Hospital administrator	SEC	1			
250.257	Insurance agent/broker	ECS	2			
119.267	Law clerk	ESA	1			
110.107	Lawyer	ESA	5	1		1
230.367	Mail carrier	CSR	1			
189.167	Management trainee	ESC			1	1
050.067	Market-research analyst	IAS	1			
— —	Medical student	—	1		1	1
152.041	Musician	ASI	1			
169.167	Office manager	ESC	2			
166.117	Personnel manager	SEC	2	1	1	2
045.107	Psychologist	SIA	1			
165.067	Public-relations practitioner	AES			1	1

DOT	JOB TITLE	HOC	1960-1974	1975-1980 M	F	T
290.477	Sales clerk	ESC	1			
163.167	Sales manager	ESC	1			
279.357	Sales/service representative	ESC	5		3	3
— —	Seminarian	—	1			
188.117	Social-welfare director	ESC	3		1	1
195.107	Social worker	SIC	2		2	2
375.167	Special agent/FBI	SRE	1			
185.167	Store manager	ESI	1			
012.167	Systems analyst/electronic data processing	ERI	1			
090.227	Teacher/college	SIA	14	1		1
092.227	Teacher/elementary	SAI	5	1		1
091.227	Teacher/high school	SAE	34		1	1
099.227	Teacher/other	SIR	10	1	1	2
094.227	Teacher/special education	SAI	1			
159.147	Television/radio personnel	AES	1			
137.267	Translator	ASI	1		1	1
			137	9	24	33

Through space the universe grasps me and swallows me up like a speck; through thought I grasp it.
                                    — *Pascal*

NATURAL SCIENCE
GENERAL DESCRIPTION

T his is a composite major which includes courses in biology, chemistry, mathematics, and physics. Students who want a broad background in several sciences usually choose this major. That way, they can keep their options open before making a commitment to professional studies or to a single science upon entering graduate school. This program also prepares students for certification to teach in elementary or secondary schools, to attend medical school, or to become involved with other health-oriented programs such as physical therapy.

A bachelor's degree equips students to enter a variety of graduate programs which include the natural sciences, medicine, law, business and finance. With appropriate electives in business, accounting, or computer science, they can also qualify for a large range of positions in business and industry as trainees, managers, or technical sales and service representatives.

Natural science majors can also find entry jobs as assistants to life scientists, medical researchers, and environmentalists. By developing effective writing skills, they can become science reporters, editors, and technical-report writers.

With advanced degrees, graduates can get into independent research, administrative positions, or teaching posts in colleges and universities.

CAREER LEADS

DOT	JOB TITLE	HOC
029.081	Air-pollution analyst	IRA
041.061	Anatomist	IRS
041.061	Animal ecologist	IRS
040.061	Animal scientist	RIS
021.067	Astronomer	IAR
041.061	Biochemist	RIS
041.061	Biophysicist	IRS
041.061	Botanist	IRS
262.357	Chemical-sales representative	ESR
079.101	Chiropractor	SIR
020.187	Computer programer	IAS
131.067	Copy writer	ASI
029.281	Crime-laboratory analyst	IRA
029.281	Criminalist	IRA
102.017	Curator/medical museum	AEI
102.017	Curator/natural history museum	AEI
041.061	Cytologist	IRS
072.101	Dentist	ISR
077.117	Dietitian	SIE
132.017	Editor/scientific publications	ASI
041.061	Entomologist	IRS
029.081	Environmental analyst	IRA
168.267	Food-and-drugs inspector	SIE
022.061	Food chemist	IAR
070.061	Forensic pathologist	ISA
040.061	Forester	RIS
045.107	Guidance counselor	SIA
187.117	Hospital administrator	SEC
024.061	Hydrologist	IRA
079.161	Industrial hygienist	SIR
045.107	Industrial psychologist	SIA
109.067	Information scientist	IRC
199.364	Laboratory assistant	ICR
029.261	Laboratory technician	IRA
110.107	Lawyer	ESA
189.167	Management trainee	ESC
141.061	Medical illustrator	ASI

DOT	JOB TITLE	HOC
100.167	Medical librarian	SAI
078.361	Medical technologist	ISR
102.381	Museum technician	AEI
078.361	Nuclear medical technologist	ISR
168.167	Occupational-safety-and-health inspector	SIE
024.061	Oceanographer	IRA
119.167	Patent examiner	ESA
022.161	Perfumer	IAR
074.161	Pharmacist	IES
076.121	Physical therapist	SIR
041.061	Plant pathologist	IRS
029.281	Police chemist	IRA
022.061	Pollution-control chemist	IAR
163.267	Product-distribution manager	ESC
189.117	Product manager	ESC
183.117	Production manager	ESC
012.167	Quality-control engineer	ERI
045.107	Rehabilitation counselor	SIA
168.264	Safety inspector	SIE
079.117	Sanitarian	SIR
040.061	Soil scientist	RIS
199.261	Taxidermist	ICR
090.227	Teacher/college	SIA
091.227	Teacher/high school	SAE
131.267	Technical writer	ASI
029.081	Water-quality analyst	IRA
025.267	Weather observer	IRA

HIRING INSTITUTIONS

Arboretums
Botanical Gardens
Business Corporations
Educational Institutions
Engineering Firms
Government Agencies
        Agriculture Department
        Airports
        Civil Service Commission
        Consumer Affairs Office
        Education Department
        Energy Department
        Environmental Protection Agency
        Federal Communications Commission
        Fish and Wildlife Services
        Government Printing Office
        Health and Human Services Department
        Library of Congress
        National Park Service
        National Science Foundation
        Nuclear Regulation Commission
        Peace Corps
        Vista
Hospitals
Libraries, Medical/Technical
Magazines, Newspapers
Manufacturing/Processing Firms
Medical Laboratories
Mining Companies
Petroleum Companies
Pharmaceutical Companies
Professional/Technical Journals
Publishing Companies
Radio/Television Stations
Research-and-Development Firms
Utility Companies

CURRENT OCCUPATIONS OF GRADUATES
WHO MAJORED IN NATURAL SCIENCE

DOT	JOB TITLE	HOC	1960-1974	1975-1980 M	F	T
160.167	Accountant	CES			1	1
188.117	Administrative officer/ government service	ESC	1			
— —	Armed services	—	5	1	1	2
041.061	Biologist	IRS	1			
189.117	Business executive	ESC	2			
186.117	Cashier/bank	ESC			1	1
022.061	Chemist	IAR	3	1		1
022.061	Chemist/research	IAR	2	2		2
079.101	Chiropractor	SIR		2		2
120.007	Clergy member	SAI	1			
209.562	Clerk	CIE	1		1	1
213.132	Computer-operations supervisor	CIS	1			
020.187	Computer programer	IAS	1	1		1
131.067	Copy writer	ASI	1			
091.267	Credit analyst	ESC		1		1
— —	Dental student	—	1	2		2
072.101	Dentist	ISR	8	1		1
189.117	General Manager	ESC	2	2	1	3
— —	Graduate student	—	8	10	6	16
045.107	Guidance counselor	SIA	2			
091.107	High-school department chairperson	SAE	1			
012.167	Industrial engineer	ERI	1	1		1
250.257	Insurance agent/broker	ECS		1		1
029.261	Laboratory technician	IRA	6	3		3
— —	Law student	—	1	1	1	2
110.107	Lawyer	ESA	3	1	1	2
230.367	Mail carrier	CSR		1		1
163.117	Marketing manager	ESC	1			
— —	Medical student	—	5	13	5	18
078.261	Medical technologist	ISR	3	1	1	2
169.167	Office manager	ESC	3			
184.167	Operations manager	ESC	1			
074.161	Pharmacist	IES	1	1		1

DOT	JOB TITLE	HOC	1960-1974	1975-1980 M	F	T
070.101	Physician	ISA	7	2		2
023.061	Physicist	IAR		1		1
079.101	Podiatrist	SIR	1			
163.267	Product-distribution manager	ESC	1			
189.117	Product manager	ESC	2			
045.107	Psychologist	SIA	1		1	1
012.167	Quality-control engineer	ERI	1	1		1
045.107	Rehabilitation counselor	SIA			1	1
290.447	Sales clerk	ESC		1		1
279.357	Sales/service representative	ESC	3	2		2
186.167	Security officer	ESC		1	1	2
600-800	Skilled trades	RIC	2			
070.101	Surgeon	ISA	1			
012.167	Systems analyst/electronic data processing	ERI	1			
092.227	Teacher/elementary school	SAI	2		1	1
091.227	Teacher/high school	SAE	10	3	2	5
099.227	Teacher/other	SIR	2		1	1
184.117	Transportation manager	ESC		1		1
199.167	Urban planner	ICR			1	1
073.101	Veterinarian	IRS	1			
			101	58	27	85

*The natural flights of the human mind are not from
pleasure to pleasure but from hope to hope.*
— *Dr. Johnson*

PHILOSOPHY
GENERAL DESCRIPTION

As a branch of learning, philosophy probes the nature of the human species and the ways people seek to understand their world. Topics that philosophers investigate include reality, perception, morality, ethics, knowledge, aesthetics, and existence.

Students of philosophy learn to analyze and evaluate, by logical processes, the premises on which we base our ideas about life.

This helps students develop flexibility in their thinking, along with the ability to apply their training to a variety of other subjects. Such reasoning skills are essential in almost every area of human endeavor: business, industry, the arts, publishing, social services, politics, or diplomacy.

Business leaders most frequently cite the ability to learn in new situations and the capacity to analyze, evaluate, and interpret data as two of the most important qualities that successful executives must possess. Still another necessary skill for success in any field is the ability to communicate clearly and effectively in speech and writing. As our technology continues its rapid expansion, these communications skills take on added importance not only to exploit our technology, but to use it judiciously.

A bachelor's degree can qualify you for trainee jobs that lead to managerial or personnel positions in business, jobs with non-profit organizations such as the Red Cross or Catholic Relief Services, and entry-level administrative posts with most government agencies.

Graduates who have refined their communications skills can become editors, reporters, or technical writers. Or they can find their way into writing and announcing jobs with radio, network, and cable TV stations.

Students frequently go on for graduate studies in law, the ministry, finance, psychological counseling, and diplomacy. Those who wish to teach in colleges will need a doctorate.

CAREER LEADS

DOT	JOB TITLE	HOC
188.117	Administrative officer/government service	ESC
055.067	Anthropological linguist	IAR
055.067	Anthropologist	IAR
101.167	Archivist	SAI
052.067	Biographer	SEI
131.067	Book critic	ASI
100.387	Cataloger	SAI
120.007	Clergy member	SAI
090.117	College/university official	SIA
131.067	Columnist/commentator	ASI
131.067	Critic (book, drama, film)	ASI
188.117	Cultural-affairs officer	ESC
102.017	Curator (art galleries, museums)	AEI
090.167	Department head/college	SIA
090.167	Director of institutional research	SIA
132.067	Editor/dictionary	ASI
132.067	Editor/publications	ASI
132.267	Editorial assistant	ASI
131.067	Editorial writer	ASI
059.067	Etymologist	SIA
131.267	Foreign correspondent	ASI
188.117	Foreign-service officer	ESC
052.067	Genealogist	SEI
168.167	Immigration inspector	SIE
250.257	Insurance agent/broker	ECS
059.267	Intelligence specialist	SIA
051.067	International-relations specialist	SIA
110.107	Lawyer	ESA
100.127	Librarian	SAI
189.167	Management trainee	ESC
132.167	Manuscript reader	ASI
102.381	Museum technician	AEI
132.067	News editor (radio, TV)	ASI
119.267	Paralegal assistant	ESA
166.117	Personnel manager	SEC
059.067	Philologist	SIA
070.101	Physician	ISA

DOT	JOB TITLE	HOC
209.387	Proofreader	CIE
070.107	Psychiatrist	ISA
045.107	Psychologist	SIA
165.067	Public-relations representative	AES
131.267	Reporter (print and publications)	ASI
109.267	Research assistant	IRC
277.357	Salesperson/books	ESC
195.107	Social worker	SIC
375.167	Special agent/FBI	SRE
090.227	Teacher/college	SIA
119.287	Title examiner	ESA
353.167	Tour guide	SRE
166.227	Training instructor	SEC
252.157	Travel agent	ECS
131.067	Writer (prose, fiction, nonfiction)	ASI

HIRING INSTITUTIONS

Archives, Federal/Municipal
Bookstores
Business Corporations
Churches and Religious Organizations
Colleges and Schools
Educational Institutions
Foundations, Non-Profit
Government Agencies
      Civil Rights Commission
      Civil Service Commission
      Consumer Affairs Office
      Education Department
      Energy Department
      Environmental Protection Agency
      Federal Communications Commission
      Foreign Service
      Government Printing Office
      Health and Human Services Department
      Labor Department
      Library of Congress
      National Archives
      National Foundations on the Arts
        and the Humanities
      Peace Corps
      Vista
Industries/Manufacturing
Insurance Companies
Learned Periodicals
Libraries
Magazines and Newspapers
Museums
Professional Periodicals
Public-Relations Firms
Publishing Companies
Radio/Television Stations
Research Institutes
Social-Service Agencies
Travel Agencies

CURRENT OCCUPATIONS OF GRADUATES WHO MAJORED IN PHILOSOPHY

DOT	JOB TITLE	HOC	1960-1974	1975-1980 M	F	T
— —	Armed services	—	1			
189.117	Business executive	ESC	2			
209.562	Clerk	CIE			1	1
020.187	Computer programer	IAS	1			
110.117	District attorney	ESA	1			
189.117	General manager	ESC	1	1		1
— —	Graduate student	—	4	1		1
186.117	Insurance-and-risk manager	ESC	1			
— —	Law student	—		1	1	2
110.107	Lawyer	ESA	5	1		1
100.117	Librarian	SAI	1			
230.367	Mail carrier	CSR	1			
189.167	Management trainee	ESC			1	1
169.167	Office manager	ESC	1			
163.167	Sales manager	ESC	1			
— —	Seminarian	—	1			
600-800	Skilled trades	RIC	1			
195.107	Social worker	SIC	4			
185.167	Store manager	ESI		1		1
003.167	Systems engineer	IRE	1			
091.227	Teacher/high school	SAE	3			
			30	5	3	8

Nature, to be commanded, must be obeyed.
— *Sir Francis Bacon*

PHYSICS
GENERAL DESCRIPTION

P hysicists analyze the structure of matter and the way it interacts with various forms of energy such as heat, light, sound, electricity, and magnetism. From their research, physicists construct theories and formulate laws to explain how the universe works.

Most physicists engage in research and development, and specialize in one or more branches of the science — such as optics, acoustics, electronics, and nuclear or plasma physics. And others combine physics with a related science such as geophysics, astrophysics, or biophysics. The basic research that physicists do often finds applications in areas they could not have foreseen: solid-state physics led to the development of transistors, and the laser beam became an instrument for surgery.

With a bachelor's degree, you can carry on applied research or develop new products for companies that manufacture defense matériel, or electrical or scientific equipment. In hospitals and other health facilities, you can also get jobs that involve working with radiation and advanced types of life-support equipment, and with firms that develop and operate computers and electronic data-processing equipment. Or you can locate with government agencies such as the Air Force, Defense, and Energy Departments, the Nuclear Regulatory Commission, the Environmental Protection Agency, the National Science Foundation, or the Goddard Space Flight Center.

Physicists who wish to conduct research projects or teach in colleges must plan to earn advanced degrees.

CAREER LEADS

DOT	JOB TITLE	HOC
002.061	Aerodynamist	IRE
196.167	Airplane navigator	IRC
196.263	Airplane pilot	IRC
001.061	Architect	AIR
021.067	Astronomer	IAR
199.267	Ballistics expert	ICR
041.061	Biophysicist	IRS
020.187	Computer programer	IAS
003.167	Computer-systems engineer	IRE
029.281	Crime laboratory analyst	IRA
029.281	Criminalist	IRA
102.017	Curator/natural history	AEI
132.067	Editor/science	ASI
132.017	Editor (technical and scientific publications)	ASI
131.067	Editorial writer	ASI
029.081	Environmental analyst	IRA
029.081	Environmental scientist	IRA
018.167	Geodetic computer	RCI
024.061	Geologist	IRA
079.021	Health physicist	SIR
024.061	Hydrologist	IRA
012.167	Industrial-health engineer	ERI
079.161	Industrial hygienist	SIR
109.067	Information scientist	IRC
022.281	Laboratory tester	IAR
110.107	Lawyer	ESA
100.127	Librarian	SAI
189.167	Management trainee	ESC
078.361	Medical technologist	ISR
011.061	Metallurgist	IRE
025.062	Meteorologist	IRA
024.061	Oceanographer	IRA
079.101	Optometrist	SIR
110.117	Patent attorney	ESA
018.261	Photogrammetrist	RCI
029.280	Photo-optics technician	IRA

DOT	JOB TITLE	HOC
029.067	Physical geographer	IRA
070.101	Physician	ISA
023.061	Physicist (acoustic, atomic, electronic heat, light, mechanic, nuclear, solid state)	IAR
023.061	Physicist/cryogenics	IAR
023.061	Physicist/plasma	IAR
023.067	Physicist/theoretical	IAR
029.281	Police chemist	IRA
078.362	Radiologic (X-ray) technologist	ISR
012.167	Safety manager	ERI
024.061	Seismologist	IRA
002.061	Stress analyst	IRE
090.227	Teacher/college	SIA
017.281	Technical illustrator	RIA
025.267	Weather observer	IRA
131.267	Writer/technical publications	ASI

HIRING INSTITUTIONS

Air, Bus, and Rail Lines
Airports
Atomic and Nuclear Laboratories
Colleges and Schools
Educational Institutions
Engineering Firms
Government Agencies
      Agriculture Department
      Commerce Department
      Consumer Affairs Office
      Energy Department
      Federal Communications Commission
      Health and Human Services Department
      National Science Foundation
      Nuclear Regulation Commission
      Peace Corps
      Vista

Hospitals
Magazines, Newspapers
Manufacturing and Processing Firms
Mining Companies
Nuclear Plants
Petroleum Companies
Professional/Technical Journals
Publishing Companies
Radio/Television Stations
Research-and-Development Firms
Utility Companies
Weather Bureaus and Companies

CURRENT OCCUPATIONS OF GRADUATES WHO MAJORED IN PHYSICS

DOT	JOB TITLE	HOC	1960-1974	1975-1980 M	F	T
160.167	Accounting manager	CES	1			
188.117	Administrative officer/ government service	ESC	1			
002.061	Aeronautical engineer	IRE	2			
— —	Armed services	—	3			
186.117	Bank officer	ESC	1			
189.117	Business executive	ESC	4	1		1
022.061	Chemist	IAR	2			
209.562	Clerk	CIE	1			
213.132	Computer-operations supervisor	CIS	3			
020.187	Computer programer	IAS	2			
003.167	Data-processing engineer	IRE	1			
— —	Dental student	—	1			
183.117	District manager	ESC	1			
003.061	Electrical engineer	IRE	7			
020.167	Financial/investment analyst	IAS	1			
189.117	General manager	ESC	1			
— —	Graduate student	—	3			
091.107	High-school department chairperson	SAE	2			

DOT	JOB TITLE	HOC	1960-1974	1975-1980		
				M	F	T
012.167	Industrial engineer	ERI	1			
376.367	Investigator	SRE	1			
110.107	Lawyer	ESA	1			
012.167	Management/methods engineer	ERI	1			
163.117	Marketing manager	ESC	2			
— —	Medical student	—	2			
169.167	Office manager	ESC	3			
184.167	Operations manager	ESC	1			
023.061	Physicist	IAR	12	1		1
189.117	Private-business owner	ESC	2			
183.117	Production manager	ESC	1			
189.117	Research-and-development director	ESC	2			
160.167	Revenue agent	CES	1			
290.477	Sales clerk	ESC	1			
012.167	Systems analyst/electronic data processing	ERI	2			
003.167	Systems engineer	IRE	3			
090.227	Teacher/college	SIA	3			
091.227	Teacher/high school	SAE	7	1		1
099.227	Teacher/other	SIR	1			
			84	3		3

The times are not so bad as they seem; they couldn't be. — *Jay Franklin*

POLITICAL SCIENCE
GENERAL DESCRIPTION

Political scientists explore the way people organize, administer, and operate the institutions that govern their society. Such specialists investigate phenomena in the areas of public opinion, political parties, elections, the uses of power, and international relations, as well as of the presidency, Congress, and the judicial system. They also trace how ideas about the rights and privileges of citizens evolved, and they develop theories about political processes.

Graduate specialties include comparative politics, international relations, political theory and behavior, public policy, and foreign-area studies.

With a bachelor's degree, you can get jobs in Federal agencies that deal with civil rights, consumer affairs, labor, and foreign relations, or you can serve as legislative assistant to Senators and Representatives. Corporations can use your skills to analyze political conditions abroad, evaluate tax proposals, and lobby for their interests in Congress. You can conduct public opinion surveys, and analyze election results for political parties, labor unions, and public interest groups.

For jobs in public relations, finance, and advertising that require oral and written presentations, you will gain a distinct advantage by developing your communications skills. Such skills will also put jobs in journalism, radio/TV reporting, and foreign correspondence within your reach.

Graduate studies can prepare you for positions in research, foreign service, college teaching, or high-level administrative posts.

CAREER LEADS

DOT	JOB TITLE	HOC
188.117	Administrative officer/government service	ESC
055.067	Anthropologist	IAR
101.167	Archivist	SAI
052.067	Biographer	SEI
131.067	Book critic	ASI
090.117	College/university official	SIA
131.067	Columnist/commentator	ASI
209.362	Congressional-district aide	CIE
188.117	Consular officer	ESC
131.267	Correspondent	ASI
131.067	Critic (book, drama, film)	ASI
188.117	Cultural-affairs officer	ESC
168.267	Customs inspector	SIE
054.067	Demographer	SIA
090.167	Department head/college	SIA
188.117	Diplomatic officer	ESC
090.167	Director of institutional research	SIA
132.067	Editor/publications	ASI
188.167	Election supervisor	ESC
131.267	Foreign correspondent	ASI
188.117	Foreign-service officer	ESC
184.117	Import-export agent	ESC
059.267	Intelligence specialist	SIA
051.067	International-relations specialist	SIA
166.167	Labor-relations representative	SEC
110.107	Lawyer	ESA
165.017	Legislative advocate	AES
165.017	Lobbyist	AES
187.117	Manager/chamber of commerce	SEC
050.067	Market-research analyst	IAS
131.267	Newscaster	ASI
119.267	Paralegal assistant	ESA
195.167	Parole officer	SIC
051.067	Political scientist	SIA
195.167	Probation/parole officer	SIC
165.067	Public-relations representative	AES
250.357	Real-estate agent/broker	ECS

DOT	JOB TITLE	HOC
131.267	Reporter (print and publications)	ASI
109.267	Research assistant	IRC
195.107	Social worker	SIC
375.167	Special agent/FBI	SRE
090.227	Teacher/college	SIA
119.287	Title examiner	ESA
353.167	Tour guide	SRE
199.167	Urban planner	ICR
131.067	Writer (prose, fiction, nonfiction)	ASI

HIRING INSTITUTIONS

Archives, Federal/Municipal
Business Corporations
Chambers of Commerce
Civic and Taxpayers' Associations
Colleges and Schools
Correctional Institutions
Court System
Educational Institutions
Government Agencies
    Civil Rights Commission
    Civil Service Commission
    Commerce Department
    Consumers Affairs Office
    Defense Department
    Education Department
    Energy Department
    Environmental Protection Agency
    Federal Bureau of Investigation
    Federal Trade Commission
    Foreign Service
    Government Printing Office
    Housing and Urban Development
    Labor Department
    Treasury Department
    Veteran's Administration
Historical Societies

Import/Export Companies
Labor Unions
Libraries
Magazines, Newspapers
Market-Research-Departments and Firms
Political-Action Committees
Political-Party Headquarters
Professional Periodicals
Public-Opinion-Research Companies
Public-Relations Firms
Radio/Television Stations
Regional-Planning Councils and Associations
Senators/Representatives/Local Officials
Social-Service Agencies

CURRENT OCCUPATIONS OF GRADUATES WHO MAJORED IN POLITICAL SCIENCE

DOT	JOB TITLE	HOC	1960-1974	1975-1980 M	F	T
160.167	Accountant	CES	1	1		1
160.167	Accounting manager	CES		1		1
188.117	Administrative officer/ government service	ESC	2			
164.117	Advertising manager	AES	1			
— —	Armed services	—	5	3		3
186.117	Bank officer	ESC	4		1	1
183.117	Branch manager	ESC	1			
189.117	Business executive	ESC	7		3	3
162.157	Buyer	ECS	2			
209.562	Clerk	CIE	1	2		2
090.167	College-department head	SIA			1	1
090.117	College/university official	SIA	1		1	1
119.267	Contract consultant	ESA	1			
094.117	Coordinator of special services/education	SAI		1		1
003.167	Development-and-planning engineer	IRE	2			
373.364	Firefighter	RSE	1			
189.117	General manager	ESC	4			

DOT	JOB TITLE	HOC	1960-1974	1975-1980 M	F	T
— —	Graduate student	—	2	4	1	5
045.107	Guidance counselor	SIA	1			
250.257	Insurance agent/broker	ECS	1			
169.167	Insurance underwriter	ESC	4	1		1
376.367	Investigator	SRE	1			
119.267	Law clerk	ESA	2			
— —	Law student	—	7	6	6	12
110.107	Lawyer	ESA	40	5		5
012.167	Management/methods engineer	ERI	1			
189.167	Management trainee	ESC	1	1		1
163.117	Marketing manager	ESC			1	1
050.067	Market-research analyst	IAS	1			
025.062	Meteorologist	IRA	1			
131.267	Newspaper reporter	ASI	1	1		1
169.167	Office manager	ESC	2			
184.167	Operations manager	ESC	2	1		1
195.167	Parole/probation officer	SIC	2	1		1
116.117	Personnel manager	SEC	3	1		1
375.263	Police officer	SRE		1		1
163.267	Product-distribution manager	ESC	1			
189.117	Product manager	ESC	1			
183.117	Production manager	ESC	1			
165.067	Public-relations practitioner	AES	1	1		1
162.157	Purchasing agent	ECS		1		1
250.357	Real-estate agent/broker	ECS	1	1		1
160.167	Revenue agent	CES	1			
290.477	Sales clerk	ESC	2			
163.167	Sales manager	ESC	1			
279.357	Sales/service representative	ESC	3	2		2
020.167	Securities analyst	IAS	1			
189.167	Security officer	ESC	1	1		1
— —	Seminarian	—	1			
600-800	Skilled trades	RIC	1	1		1
188.117	Social-welfare director	SIC		1		1

DOT	JOB TITLE	HOC	1960-1974	1975-1980		
				M	F	T
195.107	Social worker	SIC	6			
185.167	Store manager	ESI	1			
092.227	Teacher/elementary school	SAI	2	1		1
091.227	Teacher/high school	SAE	10			
099.227	Teacher/other	SIR	2			
166.227	Training specialist	SEC	1			
186.117	Trust officer/bank	ESC	1			
199.167	Urban planner	ICR	2			
045.107	Vocational counselor	SIA		1		1
131.067	Writer (fiction and nonfiction)	ASI	1			
			147	40	14	54

Life is like an onion: You peel off one layer at a time, and sometimes you weep.

— *Carl Sandburg*

PSYCHOLOGY
GENERAL DESCRIPTION

Psychologists examine the behavior of individuals in order to understand and explain how and why they act as they do. By learning about people's traits and tendencies through interviews, tests, and experiments, practitioners in this field can help their clients improve their personal adjustments. These behavioral scientists also analyze conditions that affect human behavior outside the individual — such as social, political, demographic, environmental conditions — to discover ways of improving the quality of life. Some fields in which psychologists specialize are clinical, social, counseling, experimental, physiological, personality, space, and industrial psychology.

Holders of a bachelor's degree can assist psychologists and other professionals in hospitals, rehabilitation centers, and correctional institutions. They also find jobs in business and industry doing market research, testing job applicants, or training new employees.

You need at least a master's degree for professional work in which you might administer and interpret psychological tests, counsel college students with educational or emotional problems, or help the handicapped find suitable training and employment.

With a doctorate, you can get certified to conduct private practice, and you can qualify for more responsible research and counseling positions in hospitals, clinics, and other health facilities. The largest number of Ph.D.'s work as teachers, counselors or administrators in colleges and universities, where you must have a doctorate to advance or receive tenure.

CAREER LEADS

DOT	JOB TITLE	HOC
164.117	Advertising manager	AES
052.067	Biographer	SEI
019.061	Biomedical engineer	RIE
131.067	Book critic	ASI
045.061	Child psychologist	SIA
120.007	Clergy member	SAI
090.117	College/university official	SIA
131.067	Columnist/commentator	ASI
195.167	Community-organization worker	SIC
020.187	Computer programer	IAS
188.117	Consumer-affairs director	ESC
096.121	Consumer-services consultant	SRI
131.067	Copy writer	ASI
188.117	Council-on-Aging/director	ESC
045.107	Counselor (guidance, rehabilitation, residence, vocational)	SIA
054.067	Criminologist	SIA
090.167	Department-head/college	SIA
090.167	Director of institutional research	SIA
132.067	Editor/publications	ASI
012.167	Efficiency expert	ERI
187.117	Hospital administrator	SEC
045.061	Human-factors specialist	SIA
012.167	Industrial engineer	ERI
076.167	Industrial therapist	SIR
109.067	Information scientist	IRC
166.267	Job analyst	SEC
110.107	Lawyer	ESA
189.167	Management trainee	ESC
166.117	Manager/employee welfare	SEC
050.067	Market-research analyst	IAS
076.121	Occupational therapist	SIR
054.067	Penologist	SIA
166.117	Personnel manager	SEC
070.101	Physician	ISA
166.167	Placement director	SEC
166.267	Prisoner-classification interviewer	SEC

DOT	JOB TITLE	HOC
195.167	Probation officer	SIC
070.107	Psychiatrist	ISA
055.067	Psychological anthropologist	IRA
045.107	Psychologist/clinical	SIA
045.061	Psychologist/developmental	SIA
045.061	Psychologist/engineering	SIA
045.061	Psychologist/experimental	SIA
045.107	Psychologist/industrial-organizational	SIA
045.107	Psychologist/school	SIA
045.067	Psychometrist	SIA
165.067	Public-relations representative	AES
195.167	Recreation director	SIC
076.124	Recreational therapist	SIR
109.267	Research assistant	IRC
251.257	Sales agent (psychological tests and industrial relations)	ECS
195.107	Social worker	SIC
375.167	Special agent/FBI	SRE
076.107	Speech pathologist	SIR
020.167	Statistician/applied	IAS
090.227	Teacher/college	SIA
094.227	Teacher/handicapped	SAI
094.227	Teacher/mentally retarded	SAI
131.067	Writer (prose, fiction, nonfiction)	ASI
131.267	Writer/technical publications	ASI

HIRING INSTITUTIONS

Adoption and Child Care Agencies
Advertising Departments and Agencies
Air, Bus, and Rail Lines
Business Corporations
Churches and Religious Organizations
Colleges and Schools
Community Organizations
> Recreation Departments
> YM - YWCAs
> YM - YWHAs
> Scouts, etc.

Correctional Institutions
Court System
Department Stores
Educational Institutions
Educational Periodicals
Government Agencies
> Civil Rights Commission
> Consumer Affairs Office
> Environmental Protection Agency
> Federal Communications Commission
> Foreign Service
> Health and Human Services Department
> Labor Department
> National Science Foundation
> Peace Corps
> Veteran's Administration
> Vista

Hospitals
Industries/Manufacturing
Magazines, Newspapers
Management-Consulting Firms
Market-Research Departments and Firms
Mental-Health Associations
Nursing Homes
Orphanages
Personnel Departments
Professional/Technical Journals

Public-Opinion-Research Companies
Public-Relations Firms
Publishing Companies
Research Institutes
Social-Service Agencies
Test-Development Corporations

CURRENT OCCUPATIONS OF GRADUATES WHO MAJORED IN PSYCHOLOGY

DOT	JOB TITLE	HOC	1960-1974	1975-1980 M	F	T
160.167	Accountant	CES		2	1	3
188.117	Administrative officer/ government service	ESC	1			
— —	Armed services	—	2	2		2
189.117	Business executive	ESC	2			
079.101	Chiropractor	SIR		1		1
209.562	Clerk	CIE		1	1	2
090.117	College/university official	SIA	1			
020.187	Computer programer	IAS	1			
— —	Dental student	—	1			
072.101	Dentist	ISR	1			
003.061	Electrical engineer	IRE	1			
187.167	Funeral director	SEC	1			
189.117	General manager	ESC	2	1	1	2
— —	Graduate student	—	15	13	6	19
045.107	Guidance counselor	SIA			1	1
187.117	Hospital administrator	SEC	1	1	2	3
250.257	Insurance agent/broker	ECS			1	1
241.217	Insurance-claim adjuster	CSE		1		1
241.217	Insurance-claim investigator	ESC			1	1
186.117	Insurance-and-risk manager	ESC		1		1
110.107	Lawyer	ESA		1		1
230.367	Mail carrier	CSR		1		1
189.167	Management trainee	ESC			1	1
— —	Medical student	—	3		1	1
078.261	Medical technologist	ISR			1	1
166.117	Personnel manager	SEC	1	1		1

DOT	JOB TITLE	HOC	1960-1974	1975-1980 M	F	T
070.101	Physician	ISA	1			
187.167	Private-business owner	ESC		1		1
189.117	Product manager	ESC		1	1	2
070.107	Psychoanalyst	ISA	1			
045.107	Psychologist	SIA	11	1	3	4
165.067	Public-relations practitioner	AES	1			
045.107	Rehabilitation counselor	SIA	4			
189.117	Research-and-development director	ESC	2			
163.167	Sales manager	ESC	1			
279.357	Sales/service representative	ESC	1			
600-800	Skilled trades	RIC	1			
188.117	Social-welfare director	ESC	1			
195.107	Social worker	SIC	1		5	5
076.107	Speech therapist	SIR	1			
185.167	Store manager	ESI		1		1
012.167	Systems analyst/electronic data processing	ERI	1			
003.167	Systems engineer	IRE	1			
090.227	Teacher/college	SIA	9			
092.227	Teacher/elementary school	SAI	2		2	2
091.227	Teacher/high school	SAE	2	1	2	3
099.227	Teacher/other	SIR	2	2		2
094.227	Teacher/special education	SAI		1		1
159.147	Television/radio personnel	AES		1		1
045.107	Vocational counselor	SIA	2	1	1	2
			78	36	31	67

It is easier to know man in general than to
understand one man in particular.
　　　　　　　　　　　　— *La Rouchefoucauld*

SOCIOLOGY
GENERAL DESCRIPTION

Sociologists investigate how people behave in social
groups — families, tribes, communities, and
governments. They analyze the behavior patterns of
social, political, religious, and business organizations, and how
such groups influence the total society. Sociologists also do
research to help identify the causes of social problems such as
crime, divorce, poverty, and racism.

Students can specialize in areas such as social
psychology, rural and urban sociology, criminology,
demography, gerontology, and social ecology. Besides doing
theoretical research, sociologists use their techniques to see
how well government programs such as income-assistance or
Medicare are helping people, to ascertain whether job training
is reducing unemployment, or to find out if communities
harboring toxic-waste sites have a high incidence of cancer.

With a bachelor's degree, students can get jobs doing
case work for child-welfare agencies or family courts, or they
can counsel ex-offenders, or mental patients at halfway houses.
Graduates can also get jobs in business and industry where
they can use their ability to analyze group-behavior as one
means of improving sales and services, or to predict the public's
response to radio and TV programs or printed publications.
With some training in statistics, you can get into the computer
and data-processing fields.

You will need advanced degrees to teach in college, to
hold senior positions in research and administration, or to do
consulting work.

CAREER LEADS

DOT	JOB TITLE	HOC
188.117	Administrative officer/government service	ESC
164.117	Advertising manager	AES
055.067	Anthropologist	IAR
052.067	Biographer	SEI
131.067	Book critic	ASI
120.007	Clergy member	SAI
090.117	College/university official	SIA
131.067	Columnist/commentator	ASI
195.167	Community-organization worker	SIC
188.117	Consumer-affairs director	ESC
096.121	Consumer-services consultant	SRI
131.067	Copy writer	ASI
188.117	Council-on-Aging/director	ESC
045.107	Counselor (guidance, rehabilitation, vocational)	SIA
054.067	Criminologist	SIA
054.067	Demographer	SIA
090.167	Department head/college	SIA
090.167	Director of institutional research	SIA
132.067	Editor/publications	ASI
055.067	Ethnologist	IAR
187.117	Hospital administrator	SEC
059.267	Intelligence specialist	SIA
166.167	Labor-relations representative	SEC
110.107	Lawyer	ESA
189.167	Management trainee	ESC
166.117	Manager/employee welfare	SEC
050.067	Market-research analyst	IAS
054.067	Medical sociologist	SIA
054.067	Penologist	SIA
166.117	Personnel manager	SEC
166.167	Placement director	SEC
166.267	Prisoner-classification interviewer	SEC
195.167	Probation officer	SIC
045.107	Psychologist/industrial	SIA
079.117	Public-health educator	SIR
165.067	Public-relations representative	AES

DOT	JOB TITLE	HOC
195.167	Recreation director	SIC
109.267	Research assistant	IRC
054.067	Research worker/social welfare	SIA
054.067	Rural sociologist	SIA
012.167	Safety manager	ERI
054.067	Social-problems specialist	SIA
054.067	Social ecologist	SIA
195.107	Social worker	SIC
054.067	Sociologist	SIA
020.167	Statistician/applied	IAS
090.227	Teacher/college	SIA
199.167	Urban planner	ICR
054.067	Urban sociologist	SIA
131.267	Writer/technical publications	ASI

HIRING INSTITUTIONS

Adoption and Child Care Agencies
Advertising Departments and Agencies
Business Corporations
Churches and Religious Organizations
Colleges and Schools
Community Organizations
      Recreation Department
      YM - YWCAs
      YM - YWHAs
      Scouts, etc.
Correctional Institutions
Court Systems
Educational Institutions
Educational Periodicals
Government Agencies
      Civil Rights Commission
      Civil Service Commission
      Consumer Affairs Office
      Defense Department
      Education Department
      Federal Communications Commission
      Federal Housing Administration

Federal Trade Commission
Foreign Service
Housing and Urban Development
Labor Department
National Labor Relations Board
Peace Corps
Veteran's Administration
Vista
Hospitals
Industries, Manufacturing
Labor Unions
Magazines, Newspapers
Market Research Departments and Firms
Personnel Departments
Professional Periodicals
Public-Opinion-Research Companies
Public-Relations Firms
Publishing Companies
Research Institutes
Social-Service Agencies

CURRENT OCCUPATIONS OF GRADUATES WHO MAJORED IN SOCIOLOGY

DOT	JOB TITLE	HOC	1960-1974	1975-1980 M	F	T
188.117	Administrative officer/ government service	ESC	3		1	1
— —	Armed services	—	6	1		1
153.341	Athlete	SRE	1			
160.162	Auditor	CES	2			
186.117	Bank officer	ESC	2			
183.117	Branch manager	ESC	1			
189.117	Business executive	ESC	4		1	1
162.157	Buyer	ECS	2			
022.061	Chemist/quality control	IAR	1			
079.101	Chiropractor	SIR		1		1
209.562	Clerk	CIE	4	2	1	3
090.117	College/university official	SIA	1			
213.132	Computer-operations supervisor	CIS	1			
020.187	Computer programer	IAS	5			

DOT	JOB TITLE	HOC	1960-1974	1975-1980 M	F	T
094.117	Coordinator of special services/education	SAI	1			
160.167	Cost accountant	CES	1			
168.167	Credit-and-collection manager	SIE			1	1
132.067	Editor	ASI	1			
003.061	Electrical engineer	IRE	1			
166.267	Employment interviewer	SEC	2		1	1
189.117	General manager	ESC	4	2	1	3
— —	Graduate student	—	8	1	1	2
045.107	Guidance counselor	SIA	4	1		1
091.107	High-school official	SAE	2			
052.067	Historian	SEI	1			
187.117	Hospital administrator	SEC	3		1	1
250.257	Insurance agent/broker	ECS		1		1
241.217	Insurance-claim investigator	CSE	1			
186.117	Insurance-and-risk manager	ESC		1		1
169.167	Insurance underwriter	ESC	1			
376.367	Investigator	SRE		1		1
166.167	Labor-relations consultant	SEC	1			
119.267	Law clerk	ESA	1			
110.107	Lawyer	ESA	8	1		1
100.127	Librarian	SAI	1			
230.367	Mail carrier	CSR		1		1
189.167	Management trainee	ESC	1			
163.117	Marketing manager	ESC	2	1		1
— —	Medical student	—	1			
169.167	Office manager	ESC	3	1		1
184.167	Operations manager	ESC	1			
195.167	Parole/probation officer	SIC	6			
166.117	Personnel manager	SEC	5		2	2
070.101	Physician	ISA	3			
196.263	Pilot/airplane	IRC	1			
183.117	Production manager	ESC	2		1	1
070.107	Psychiatrist	ISA	1			
045.107	Psychologist	SIA	4			
165.067	Public-relations practitioner	AES	2			

DOT	JOB TITLE	HOC	1960-1974	1975-1980		
				M	F	T
162.157	Purchasing agent	ECS	1	1		1
250.357	Real-estate agent/broker	ECS	1			
045.107	Rehabilitation counselor	SIA	1			
189.117	Research-and-development director	ESC	1			
290.477	Sales clerk	ESC	1	1	1	2
163.167	Sales manager	ESC	1			
279.357	Sales/service representative	ESC	8	1		1
186.167	Securities trader	ESC	1			
189.167	Security officer	ESC	1			
188.117	Social-welfare director	ESC	1			
195.107	Social worker	SIC	23	2	4	6
054.067	Sociologist	SIA	1			
020.167	Statistician	IAS			1	1
251.157	Stockbroker	ECS	1			
185.167	Store manager	ESI	1			
012.167	Systems analyst/electronic data processing	ERI	4			
090.227	Teacher/college	SIA	10	1		1
092.227	Teacher/elementary school	SAI	6		3	3
091.227	Teacher/high school	SAE	10	3	1	4
099.227	Teacher/other	SIR	9		1	1
159.147	Television/radio personnel	AES	1			
166.227	Training specialist	SEC	1			
184.117	Transportation manager	ESC		1		1
199.167	Urban planner	ICR	4		1	1
045.107	Vocational counselor	SIA	1			
131.067	Writer (fiction and nonfiction)	ASI	1			
			196	25	23	48

He conquers who endures.   *— Persius*

URBAN STUDIES
GENERAL DESCRIPTION

Urban Studies concerns itself with the history, expression, and evaluation of the way people live in cities. Students in this field study the cultural resources of the city, together with such problems as poverty, violence, and crime which affect the quality of urban living. They also explore the way ethnic groups, social classes, and politics influence community planning and social reform.

Depending on their personalities and individual preferences, graduates can enter a variety of fields that relate to urban concerns. If you enjoy direct contact with people, you can either teach or perform social services — within a court system, for example, or at a correctional facility.

Perhaps you prefer managerial work. For that, you can look into hospital administration, or activities dealing with city life — such as community relations programs — that business and financial organizations sponsor.

And graduates striving to improve our physical environment can work for engineering firms that design subways and parking facilities, or for urban renewal agencies that rehabilitate schools, housing, shopping centers, and playgrounds.

With a bachelor's degree, students can find entry-level jobs in urban administration and planning, private social agencies, community-organization projects, and social welfare. They can also go on to graduate studies in urban and regional planning, architecture or law. A master's degree will qualify individuals to get a start as urban and regional planners at local, State, and Federal levels. With an additional range of experience, you can do consulting work for land-developers, engineering firms, research organizations, or government agencies.

CAREER LEADS

DOT	JOB TITLE	HOC
188.117	Administrative officer/government service	ESC
001.061	Architect	AIR
131.067	Book critic	ASI
188.117	City manager	ESC
090.117	College/university official	SIA
195.167	Community-organization worker	SIC
096.121	Consumer-services consultant	SRI
169.167	Contact representative	ESC
119.267	Contract consultant	ESA
188.117	Council-on-Aging/director	ESC
054.067	Demographer	SIA
188.167	Election supervisor	ESC
165.117	Fund-raising director	AES
188.167	Director of vital statistics	ESC
099.117	Educational-program director	SIE
166.267	Employment interviewer	SEC
001.061	Environmental planner	AIR
187.117	Hospital administrator	SEC
188.117	Housing-management officer	ESC
166.267	Job analyst	SEC
166.167	Labor-relations representative	SEC
110.107	Lawyer	ESA
165.017	Lobbyist	AES
161.167	Management analyst	CES
189.167	Management trainee	ESC
187.117	Manager/chamber of commerce	SEC
166.117	Manager/employee welfare	SEC
166.067	Occupational analyst	SEC
169.167	Office manager	ESC
119.267	Paralegal assistant	ESA
166.267	Prisoner-classification interviewer	SEC
195.167	Probation officer	SIC
165.067	Public-relations representative	SIR
162.157	Purchasing agent	ECS
250.357	Real-estate agent/broker	ECS
195.167	Recreation director	SIC
131.267	Reporter (print and publications)	ASI

DOT	JOB TITLE	HOC
012.167	Safety manager	ERI
195.117	Social-welfare director	SIC
195.107	Social worker	SIC
090.227	Teacher/college	SIA
119.287	Title examiner	ESA
184.167	Transportation manager	ESC
199.167	Urban planner	ICR
054.067	Urban sociologist	SIA

HIRING INSTITUTIONS

Adoption and Child Care Agencies
Business Corporations
Chambers of Commerce
Civic and Taxpayers' Associations
Colleges and Schools
Community Organizations

> Recreation Departments
> YM - YWCAs
> YM - YWHAs
> Scouts, etc.

Correctional Institutions
Court Systems
Educational Institutions
Government Agencies

> Civil Rights Commission
> Civil Service Commission
> Consumer Affairs Office
> Education Department
> Environmental Protection Agency
> Federal Housing Administration
> Federal Labor Relations Board
> Federal Trade Commission
> Foreign Service
> Health and Human Services Department
> Housing and Urban Development

> Labor Department
> Peace Corps
> Veteran's Administration
> Vista

Hospitals
Housing Authorities
Industries, Manufacturing
Labor Unions
Libraries
Magazines, Newspapers
Municipalities
Professional Periodicals
Public-Relations Firms
Regional Planning Councils and
   Associations
Social-Service Agencies
Urban-Renewal Agencies

CURRENT OCCUPATIONS OF GRADUATES WHO MAJORED IN URBAN STUDIES

DOT	JOB TITLE	HOC	1960-1974	1975-1980 M	F	T
160.167	Accounting manager	CES	1			
188.117	Administrative officer/ government service	ESC	2	2	1	3
— —	Armed services	—	2	1		1
160.162	Auditor	CES		1		1
186.117	Bank officer	ESC			2	2
161.117	Budget analyst	CES	3			
189.117	Business executive	ESC	1		1	1
120.007	Clergy member	SAI	2			
209.562	Clerk	CIE	1	1	2	3
119.267	Contract consultant	ESA		1		1
191.267	Credit analyst	ESC			1	1
187.167	Funeral director	SEC		1		1
189.117	General manager	ESC	3			
— —	Graduate student	—		1	5	6

DOT	JOB TITLE	HOC	1960-1974	1975-1980		
				M	F	T
045.107	Guidance counselor	SIA			1	1
187.117	Hospital administrator	SEC	2			
187.117	Hotel/restaurant manager	SEC	1			
250.257	Insurance agent/broker	ECS	1	1		1
376.367	Investigator	SRE			1	1
166.167	Labor-relations consultant	SEC			1	1
119.267	Law clerk	ESA	2			
— —	Law student	—			1	1
110.107	Lawyer	ESA	2			
230.367	Mail carrier	CSR	1			
131.267	Newspaper reporter	ASI		1		1
169.167	Officer manager	ESC	3		2	2
166.267	Personnel manager	SEC			1	1
375.263	Police officer	SRE	1	1		1
183.117	Production manager	ESC	1			
045.107	Psychologist	SIA			1	1
165.067	Public-relations practitioner	AES			1	1
162.157	Purchasing agent	ECS	1	1		1
250.357	Real-estate agent/broker	ECS	1			
189.117	Research-and-development director	ESC	1		1	1
290.477	Sales clerk	ESC	1			
163.167	Sales manager	ESC		1		1
279.357	Sales/service representative	ESC			1	1
189.167	Security officer	ESC	1			
600-800	Skilled trades	RIC	1	1		1
188.117	Social-welfare director	ESC	1		3	3
195.107	Social worker	SIC	5		6	6
251.157	Stockbroker	ECS		1		1
012.167	Systems analyst/electronic data processing	ERI	1			
090.227	Teacher/college	SIA	3			
092.227	Teacher/elementary school	SAI	1			
091.227	Teacher/high school	SAE	1			
099.227	Teacher/other	SIR	1	1	1	2
184.117	Transportation manager	ECS		1		1
199.167	Urban planner	ICR	1	1		1
045.107	Vocational counselor	SIA	3		1	1
			52	18	34	52

PART FIVE

JOB INDEX: MAJOR OF GRADUATES BY OCCUPATION

A book without an index is much like a compass-box without the needle, perplexing instead of directive to the point we would reach. — Anon.

PART FIVE
THE MAJORS OF GRADUATES —
BY OCCUPATION

DOT	JOB TITLE	HOC	1960-1974	1975-1980 M	F	T
160.167	**Accountant**	CES				
	Accountancy		249	218	50	268
	Biology		1	1		1
	Economics		15	5		5
	English		1	1		1
	History		5	2		2
	Management		16	18	2	20
	Marketing		11	3	2	5
	Math/Computer Science		2			
	Natural Science				1	1
	Political Science		1	1		1
	Psychology			2	1	3
			301	251	56	307
160.167	**Accounting Manager**	CES				
	Accountancy		41	11	3	14
	Economics		4			
	English		1			
	History		2	1		1
	Management		6	2	3	5
	Marketing		2	1	1	2
	Math/Computer Science		3			
	Modern Languages		1			
	Physics		1			
	Political Science			1		1
	Urban Studies		1			
			62	16	7	23
160.167	**Accounting Partner**	CES				
	Accountancy		17	4		4
	Management		1			
			18	4		4

DOT	JOB TITLE	HOC	1960-1974	1975-1980 M	F	T
150.047	**Actor**	ASE				
	Biology			1		1
	Classics		1			
	English		1	1		1
	Marketing		1			
	Modern Languages		1			
			4	2		2
020.167	**Actuary**	IAS				
	Management		1			
	Marketing				1	1
	Math/Computer Science		8	1	1	2
			9	1	2	3
169.167	**Administrative Officer Government Service/**	ESC				
	Accountancy		9			
	Art History		1			
	Chemistry		2			
	Classics		2			
	Economics		20			
	Education		1			
	English		8	2		2
	History		8			
	Management		19	3	2	5
	Marketing		21	1	1	2
	Math/Computer Science		3			
	Modern Languages		3			
	Natural Science		1			
	Physics		1			
	Political Science		2			
	Psychology		1			
	Sociology		3		1	1
	Urban Studies		2	2	1	3
			107	8	5	13

DOT	JOB TITLE	HOC	1960-1974	1975-1980 M	F	T
164.117	**Advertising Manager**	AES				
	Accountancy		2			
	Economics		1			
	Education				1	1
	English		1		2	2
	History		2			
	Management		4	1		1
	Marketing		2	1		1
	Political Science		1			
			13	2	3	5
002.061	**Aeronautical Engineer**	IRE				
	Physics		2			
			2			
070.101	**Anesthesiologist** .... (see Medical Doctor)	ISA				
001.061	**Architect**	AIR				
	History			1		1
				1		1
— —	**Armed Services**	—				
	Accountancy		16	2	1	3
	Biology		13	2		2
	Chemistry		7			
	Classics		1			
	Economics		24	1		1
	Education		1			
	English		19	2		2
	History		37	7		7
	Management		17	8		8

DOT	JOB TITLE	HOC	1960-1974	1975-1980 M	F	T
	Marketing		18			
	Math/Computer Science		12			
	Modern Languages		5	1		1
	Natural Science		5	1	1	2
	Philosophy		1			
	Physics		3			
	Political Science		5	3		3
	Psychology		2	2		2
	Sociology		6	1		1
	Urban Studies		2	1		1
			194	31	2	33
144.061	**Artist** .... AIR					
	Art History		2			
	English		1		1	1
	Marketing			1		1
			3	1	1	2
153.341	**Athlete** .... SRE					
	Sociology		1			
			1			
099.167	**Audiovisual Specialist** .... SIE					
	Art History		1			
	Management		1			
			1			
160.162	**Auditor** .... CES					
	Accountancy		69	40	7	47
	Classics		1			
	Economics		8	1		1

DOT	JOB TITLE	HOC	1960-1974	1975-1980 M	F	T
	History		2	1		1
	Management		11	4		4
	Marketing		5	1		1
	Math/Computer Science		1	1		1
	Sociology		2			
	Urban Studies			1		1
			99	49	7	56
186.117	**Bank Officer**	ESC				
	Accountancy		24	9	6	15
	Economics		47	2	1	3
	English		6			
	History		16	1		1
	Management		46	19	5	24
	Math/Computer Science		8			
	Marketing		24	3	1	4
	Modern Languages		4	1	1	2
	Physics		1			
	Political Science		4		1	1
	Sociology		2			
	Urban Studies				2	2
			182	35	17	52
041.061	**Biochemist**	IRS				
	Biology		1	1		1
			1	1		1
041.061	**Biologist**	IRS				
	Biology		3	1		1
	Natural Science		1			
			4	1		1

DOT	JOB TITLE	HOC	1960-1974	1975-1980 M	F	T
183.117	**Branch Manager**	ESC				
	Accountancy		1	3		3
	Chemistry		1			
	Economics		3			
	History		2			
	Management		10	3		3
	Marketing		4			
	Math/Computer Science		1			
	Political Science		1			
	Sociology		1			
			24	6		6
186.117	**Brokerage-House Partner**	ESC				
	Accountancy				1	1
	Economics		1			
			1		1	1
161.117	**Budget Analyst**	CES				
	Accountancy		7	2	1	3
	Economics		4		1	1
	History			1		1
	Management		5	4	2	6
	Marketing		6			
	Math/Computer Science		1	1		1
	Modern Languages		1			
	Urban Studies		3			
			27	8	4	12
189.117	**Business Executive**	ESC				
	Accountancy		113	7		7
	Art History		1	1		1
	Biology		1	2		2

DOT	JOB TITLE	HOC	1960-1974	1975-1980 M	F	T
	Chemistry		5		1	1
	Classics		2		1	1
	Economics		43	4		4
	Education		1		3	3
	English		29		2	2
	History		20	3		3
	Managment		52	12	5	17
	Marketing		45	7	2	9
	Math/Computer Science		15	1	1	2
	Modern Languages		4		1	1
	Natural Science		2			
	Philosophy		2			
	Physics		4	1		1
	Political Science		7		3	3
	Psychology		2			
	Sociology		4		1	1
	Urban Studies		1		1	1
			353	38	21	59
162.157	**Buyer**	ECS				
	Accountancy		1	1		1
	Art History		1			
	Economics		2			
	English		3	1		1
	History		2			
	Management		6	3	2	5
	Marketing		10	1	2	3
	Modern Languages		1			
	Political Science		2			
	Sociology		2			
			30	6	4	10

DOT	JOB TITLE	HOC	1960-1974	1975-1980 M	F	T
186.117	**Cashier, Bank**	ESC				
	Accountancy				1	1
	Economics		3			
	History		2			
	Management		2	3	2	5
	Marketing		4	1		1
	Natural Science				1	1
			11	4	4	8
022.061	**Chemist**	IAR				
	Biology		5	3	2	5
	Chemistry		33	4	3	7
	Economics			1		1
	Math/Computer Science			1		1
	Natural Science		3	1		1
	Physics		2			
			43	10	5	15
022.061	**Chemist, Analytical**	IAR				
	Biology			2		2
	Chemistry		2			
			2	2		2
022.061	**Chemist/ Quality Control**	IAR				
	Biology		1	1	1	2
	Chemistry		1			
	Economics			1		1
	English		1			
	Sociology		1			
			4	2	1	3

DOT	JOB TITLE	HOC	1960-1974	1975-1980 M	F	T
022.061	**Chemist/Research**	IAR				
	Biology		3	1	1	2
	Chemistry		18			
	Management		1			
	Math/Computer Science		1			
	Natural Science		2	2		2
			25	**3**	**1**	**4**
079.101	**Chiropractor**	SIR				
	Biology		1	1		1
	Management		1			
	Modern Languages		1			
	Natural Science			2		2
	Psychology			1		1
	Sociology			1		1
			3	**5**		**5**
110.117	**Claim Attorney**	ESA				
	Economics		1			
	Business Management				1	1
			1		**1**	**1**
120.007	**Clergy Member**	SAI				
	Accountancy		1	1		1
	Art History		1			
	Biology		1			
	Chemistry			1		1
	Economics		1			
	English		1			
	History		4			
	Management		3			
	Math/Computer Science		1			

DOT	JOB TITLE	HOC	1960-1974	1975-1980		
				M	F	T
	Modern Languages		2	1		1
	Natural Science		1			
	Urban Studies		2			
			18	3		3
209.562	**Clerk** .... CIE					
	Accountancy		5	8	4	12
	Art History				1	1
	Biology		2	2	2	4
	Economics		3	3		3
	Education		1		8	8
	English		9	7	5	12
	History		4			
	Management		12	12	7	19
	Marketing		6	11	3	14
	Math/Computer Science		2	2	1	3
	Modern Languages				5	5
	Natural Science		1		1	1
	Philosophy				1	1
	Physics		1			
	Political Science		1	2		2
	Psychology			1	1	2
	Sociology		4	2	1	3
	Urban Studies		1	1	2	3
			52	51	42	93
090.167	**College Department Head** .... SIA					
	Modern Languages		1	1		1
	Political Science				1	1
			1	1	1	2

DOT	JOB TITLE	HOC	1960-1974	1975-1980 M	F	T
090.117	**College/University Official**	SIA				
	Art History				1	1
	Biology		1			
	Chemistry		1			
	Classics		2			
	Economics		2			
	Education		1		2	2
	English		6		1	1
	History		11	1		1
	Management		2	1		1
	Marketing		2			
	Math/Computer Science		1		1	1
	Modern Languages		3			
	Political Science		1		1	1
	Psychology		1			
	Sociology		1			
			35	2	6	8
213.362	**Computer Operator**	CIS				
	Accountancy		1			
	Economics		2	1		1
	English			1		1
	History		1	1		1
	Management		2		2	2
	Marketing		4	5	1	6
	Math/Computer Science		1	3		3
			11	11	3	14
213.132	**Computer-Operations Supervisor**	CIS				
	Accountancy		6	1		1
	Chemistry		1			
	Economics		8	1		1
	Education		1		1	1

DOT	JOB TITLE	HOC	1960-1974	1975-1980 M	F	T
	English		1			
	History		1			
	Management		4	8		8
	Marketing		1			
	Math/Computer Science		10	1	3	4
	Natural Science		1			
	Physics		3			
	Sociology		1			
			38	11	4	15
020.187	**Computer Programer** ..... IAS					
	Accountancy		2	4	1	5
	Biology		2	1	2	3
	Chemistry		1			
	Classics		1			
	Economics		6	3		3
	Education		1	1		1
	English		1	1		1
	History		7		1	1
	Management		21	24	2	26
	Marketing		7	10	1	11
	Math/Computer Science		45	17	9	26
	Natural Science		1	1		1
	Philosophy		1			
	Physics		2			
	Psychology		1			
	Sociology		5			
			104	62	16	78
869.664	**Construction Worker** ..... REI					
	Accountancy		1			
	Biology			1		1
	English		1			

DOT	JOB TITLE	HOC	1960-1974	1975-1980 M	F	T
	History			1	1	2
	Management		1	2		2
	Marketing		2			
			5	4	1	5
119.267	**Contract Consultant**	ESA				
	Economics		2			
	English		1	1	1	2
	Management		1			
	Math/Computer Science		1			
	Modern Languages				1	1
	Political Science		1			
	Urban Studies			1		1
			6	2	2	4
182.167	**Contractor**	ERI				
	History		1			
			1			
094.117	**Coordinator of Special Studies/ Education**	SAI				
	Biology		1			
	Chemistry		1			
	Economics		2			
	Education		2	1		1
	History		6			
	Management		1			
	Marketing		3			
	Political Science			1		1
	Sociology		1			
			17	2		2

DOT	JOB TITLE	HOC	1960-1974	1975-1980		
				M	F	T
131.067	**Copy Writer**	ASI				
	Modern Languages		1			
	Natural Science		1			
			2			
110.117	**Corporate Counsel**	ESA				
	Economics		1			
	English		1			
	History		4			
			6			
160.167	**Cost Accountant**	CES				
	Accountancy		13	7	1	8
	Economics		1		1	1
	History		1			
	Management		8	1		1
	Marketing		2			
	Math/Computer Science		1			
	Sociology		1			
			27	8	2	10
160.267	**Cost Estimator**	CES				
	Accountancy		1			
	Economics		2			
	History		1			
	Management		1	2		2
	Math/Computer Science				1	1
			5	2	1	3
191.267	**Credit Analyst**	ESC				
	Accountancy		2	2		2
	Economics		2	2	1	3
	History		1	1		1

DOT	JOB TITLE	HOC	1960-1974	1975-1980 M	F	T
	Management		2	3	1	4
	Marketing		2	1		1
	Natural Science			1		1
	Urban Studies				1	1
			9	10	3	13
168.167	**Credit-and-Collection Manager** .... SIE					
	Accountancy		2	1	1	2
	Economics		2	1		1
	Education		1			
	English			1		1
	History		2			
	Management		5	3	2	5
	Marketing		4	2		2
	Math/Computer Science		3			
	Sociology				1	1
			19	8	4	12
188.167	**Customs Officer** .... ESC					
	Economics		1			
	History		2			
	Management		1	1		1
	Math/Computer Science		1			
	Modern Languages		1			
			6	1		1
003.167	**Data-Processing Engineer** .... IRE					
	Economics		1			
	Math/Computer Science		1	1		1
	Physics		1			
			3	1		1

DOT	JOB TITLE	HOC	1960-1974	1975-1980 M	F	T
— —	**Dental Student**	—				
	Biology		2	4		4
	Chemistry			2		2
	History		1			
	Natural Science		1	2		2
	Physics		1			
	Psychology		1			
			6	8		8
072.101	**Dentist**	ISR				
	Biology		35	3	1	4
	Chemistry		5			
	Natural Science		8	1		1
	Psychology		1			
			49	4	1	5
003.167	**Development-and-Planning Engineer**	IRE				
	Accountancy		2			
	Economics		2			
	English		2			
	History		1			
	Management		4	2		2
	Marketing		3			
	Math/Computer Science		6	1	1	2
	Natural Science			1		1
	Political Science		2			
			22	4	1	5
110.117	**District Attorney**	ESA				
	Accountancy		1			
	Economics		1			
	English		2			

DOT	JOB TITLE	HOC	1960-1974	1975-1980 M	F	T
	History		2			
	Philosophy		1			
			7			
183.117	**District Manager** .... ESC					
	Accountancy		2	2		2
	Chemistry		2			
	Classics		1			
	Economics		9		1	1
	English		3			
	History		2			
	Management		7	3		3
	Marketing		9	1		1
	Math/Computer Science		3			
	Physics		1			
			39	6	1	7
050.067	**Economist** .... IAS					
	Economics		6		1	1
	History		1			
	Management		1			
	Marketing		2		1	1
	Math/Computer Science		1			
			11		2	2
050.067	**Economist/Price** .... IAS					
	Accountancy		1			
	Management			1		1
	Marketing		1			
			2	1		1

DOT	JOB TITLE	HOC	1960-1974	1975-1980 M	F	T
132.067	**Editor**	ASI				
	Classics			1		1
	English		7		2	2
	History		1			
	Management		1			
	Marketing		1		1	1
	Modern Languages		2			
	Sociology		1			
			13	1	3	4
003.061	**Electrical Engineer**	IRE				
	Economics		2	1		1
	Managment		4	2		2
	Math/Computer Science		2		1	1
	Physics		7			
	Psychology		1			
	Sociology		1			
			17	3	1	4
092.137	**Elementary-School Official**	SAI				
	Biology		1			
	Chemistry		1			
	Education		1			
	History		2			
	Management		1			
	Math/Computer Science		1			
			7			
166.267	**Employment Interviewer** ...	SEC				
	English		1		1	1
	History		2			
	Management		2			

DOT	JOB TITLE	HOC	1960-1974	1975-1980		
				M	F	T
	Marketing				1	1
	Sociology		2		1	1
			7		3	3
041.061	**Endocrinologist**	IRS				
	Biology		1			
			1			
186.167	**Estate Planner**	ESC				
	History		5			
			5			
828.261	**Field Engineer**	RIC				
	Accountancy		1			
			1			
020.167	**Financial/Investment Analyst**	IAS				
	Accountancy		27		1	1
	Economics		15	1		1
	English		4		1	1
	History		4			
	Management		3	1		1
	Marketing		8	1		1
	Math/Computer Science		3			
	Physics		1			
			65	3	2	5
050.067	**Financial Planner**	IAS				
	Accountancy		18	8	1	9
	Classics			1		1
	Economics		4			

DOT	JOB TITLE	HOC	1960-1974	1975-1980		
				M	F	T
	English		1		1	1
	History				1	1
	Management		5	2	3	5
	Marketing		1		1	1
	Math/Computer Science				1	1
			29	11	8	19
373.364	**Firefighter** .... RSE					
	Accountancy			1		1
	Economics			1		1
	English		2			
	History		2	1		1
	Management		2	2		2
	Marketing		1			
	Political Science		1			
			8	5		5
187.167	**Funeral Director** .... SEC					
	Management			1	1	2
	Marketing		1			
	Psychology		1			
	Urban Studies			1		1
			2	2	1	3
189.117	**General Manager** .... ESC					
	Accountancy		28	4	1	5
	Biology		2			
	Chemistry		1			
	Classics		1			
	Economics		24	3		3
	Education		1		2	2
	English		8	4	1	5
	History		15	1		1

DOT	JOB TITLE	HOC	1960-1974	1975-1980 M	F	T
	Management		45	37	5	42
	Marketing		24	2	2	4
	Math/Computer Science		13	1		1
	Modern Languages		1		1	1
	Natural Science		2	2	1	3
	Philosophy		1	1		1
	Physics		1			
	Political Science		4			
	Psychology		2	1	1	2
	Sociology		4	2	1	3
	Urban Studies		3			
			180	58	15	73
— —	**Graduate Student**	—				
	Accountancy		3	2		2
	Art History		1		1	1
	Biology		20	22	10	32
	Chemistry		10	3	3	6
	Classics		4	1		1
	Economics		14	1	1	2
	Education		2	1	1	2
	English		19	3	3	6
	History		21	9	1	10
	Management		5	1	1	2
	Marketing		3	1		1
	Math/Computer Science		11	1	2	3
	Modern Languages		4		1	1
	Natural Science		8	10	6	16
	Philosophy		4	1		1
	Physics		3			
	Political Science		2	4	1	5
	Psychology		15	13	6	19
	Sociology		8	1	1	2
	Urban Studies			1	5	6
			157	75	43	118

DOT	JOB TITLE	HOC	1960-1974	1975-1980 M	F	T
045.107	**Guidance Counselor**	SIA				
	Accountancy		2			
	Art History				1	1
	Classics		1			
	Economics		4			
	Education		1			
	English		2			
	History		5		1	1
	Management		2			
	Marketing		2			
	Math/Computer Science		2			
	Modern Languages				1	1
	Natural Science		2			
	Political Science		1			
	Psychology				1	1
	Sociology		4	1		1
	Urban Studies				1	1
			28	1	5	6
091.107	**High-School Department Chairperson**	SAE				
	English		3			
	History		6			
	Management		1			
	Marketing		1			
	Math/Computer Science		2			
	Natural Science		1			
	Physics		2			
			16			
091.107	**High-School Official**	SAE				
	Accountancy		2			
	Biology		1			
	Economics		3			

DOT	JOB TITLE	HOC	1960-1974	1975-1980 M	F	T
	English		3		1	1
	History		7			
	Management		2			
	Marketing		1			
	Math/Computer Science		3			
	Modern Languages		1			
	Sociology		2			
			25		1	1
052.067	**Historian**	SEI				
	Sociology		1			
			1			
040.061	**Horticulturist**	RIS				
	Biology		1			
			1			
187.117	**Hospital Administrator** ...	SEC				
	Accountancy		4			
	Biology		3			
	Chemistry			1		1
	Economics		4			
	English				1	1
	History		5			
	Management		1	1	2	3
	Modern Languages		1			
	Psychology		1	1	2	3
	Sociology		3		1	1
	Urban Studies		2			
			24	3	6	9

DOT	JOB TITLE	HOC	1960-1974	1975-1980		
				M	F	T
187.117	**Hotel/Restaurant Manager**	SEC				
	English		1			
	History		1			
	Marketing			1		1
	Urban Studies		1			
			3	1		1
012.167	**Industrial Engineer**	ERI				
	English		1		1	1
	History		2			
	Management		9	2	2	4
	Marketing		2	2		2
	Natural Science		1	1		1
	Physics		1			
			16	5	3	8
250.257	**Insurance-Agent/Broker** ..	ECS				
	Accountancy		7	1		1
	Economics		7			
	Education		1			
	English		6			
	History		7	1		1
	Management		16	6		6
	Marketing		8	1	2	3
	Math/Computer Science		5			
	Modern Languages		2			
	Natural Science			1		1
	Political Science		1			
	Psychology				1	1
	Sociology			1		1
	Urban Studies		1	1		1
			61	12	3	15

DOT	JOB TITLE	HOC	1960-1974	1975-1980		
				M	F	T
241.217	**Insurance-Claim Adjuster**	CSE				
	Accountancy		1			
	Economics		1			
	English		3		1	1
	History		1	1		1
	Management		4	5		5
	Marketing		1	2		2
	Psychology			1		1
			11	9	1	10
168.267	**Insurance-Claim Examiner**	SIE				
	Accountancy		1			
	Biology		1			
	Economics		4			
	English		3		1	1
	History		7	1	2	3
	Management		6	2	2	4
	Marketing		6			
	Math/Computer Science		1			
			29	3	5	8
241.217	**Insurance-Claim Investigator**	CSE				
	Education			1		1
	Management		2	1		1
	Marketing		1			
	Psychology				1	1
	Sociology		1			
			4	2	1	3

DOT	JOB TITLE	HOC	1960-1974	1975-1980 M	F	T
186.117	**Insurance-and-Risk Manager**	ESC				
	Economics		1			
	Management		1	1		1
	Math/Computer Science		1	1		1
	Philosophy		1			
	Psychology			1		1
	Sociology			1		1
			4	**4**		**4**
169.167	**Insurance Underwriter**	ESC				
	Accountancy		2		1	1
	Economics		3	2		2
	English		3			
	History		8	1		1
	Management		14	1		1
	Math/Computer Science		3			
	Marketing		4	1		1
	Political Science		4	1		1
	Sociology		1			
			42	**6**	**1**	**7**
142.051	**Interior Designer/ Decorator**	AIS				
	Management		1			
			1			
376.367	**Investigator**	SRE				
	Accountancy		1			
	Economics		2			
	History		2	1		1

DOT	JOB TITLE	HOC	1960-1974	1975-1980 M	F	T
	Management		3	1		1
	Physics		1			
	Political Science		1			
	Sociology			1		1
	Urban Studies				1	1
			10	**3**	**1**	**4**
111.107	**Judge**	ESA				
	Management		1			
	Economics		1			
	History		1			
			3			
022.137	**Laboratory Supervisor**	IAR				
	Chemistry		2			
	Economics		1			
			3			
029.261	**Laboratory Technician**	IRA				
	Biology		5	9	2	11
	Chemistry		1			
	Education		1			
	English				1	1
	History		2			
	Management			1		1
	Math/Computer Science			1		1
	Natural Science		6	3		3
			15	**14**	**3**	**17**
166.167	**Labor-Relations Consultant**	SEC				
	Accountancy		1			
	English		1			
	Management		1		1	1

DOT	JOB TITLE	HOC	1960-1974	1975-1980 M	F	T
	Sociology		1			
	Urban Studies				1	1
			4		2	2
119.267	**Law Clerk** .... ESA					
	Classics		1			
	Economics		1			
	English		1		1	1
	History		4	3		3
	Management		2	1		1
	Marketing			1		1
	Modern Languages		1			
	Political Science		2			
	Sociology		1			
	Urban Studies		2			
			15	5	1	6
110.107	**Law-School Professor** ..... SIA					
	English		2			
			2			
— —	**Law Student** .... —					
	Accountancy			2		2
	Biology			2		2
	Chemistry		1	1		1
	Classics		1	1		1
	Economics		3	2		2
	Education			3	1	4
	English		4		2	2
	History		15	2	2	4
	Management			3		3
	Marketing		2	1		1

DOT	JOB TITLE	HOC	1960-1974	1975-1980 M	F	T
	Math/Computer Science		1		2	2
	Natural Science		1	1	1	2
	Philosophy			1	1	2
	Political Science		7	6	6	12
	Urban Studies				1	1
			35	25	16	41
110.107	**Lawyer**	ESA				
	Accountancy		18			
	Art History				1	1
	Biology		2			
	Chemistry		1			
	Classics		14	1		1
	Economics		38			
	English		32	1		1
	History		72	4	3	7
	Management		6		1	1
	Marketing		15			
	Math/Computer Science		5			
	Modern Languages		5	1		1
	Natural Science		3	1	1	2
	Philosophy		5	1		1
	Physics		1			
	Political Science		40	5		5
	Psychology			1		1
	Sociology		8	1		1
	Urban Studies		2			
			267	16	6	22
100.127	**Librarian**	SAI				
	Economics		1			
	English		6		4	4
	History		5		2	2

DOT	JOB TITLE	HOC	1960-1974	1975-1980 M	F	T
	Management				1	1
	Marketing			2		2
	Math/Computer Science		1			
	Philosophy		1			
	Sociology		1			
			15	2	7	9
230.367	**Mail Carrier** .... CSR					
	Accountancy			2		2
	Economics		1			
	Management		2		1	1
	Marketing		1	1		1
	Modern Languages		1			
	Natural Science			1		1
	Philosophy		1			
	Psychology			1		1
	Sociology			1		1
	Urban Studies		1			
			7	6	1	7
012.167	**Management/Methods Engineer** .... ERI					
	Accountancy		1			
	Biology		1			
	Management		6			
	Marketing		2			
	Math/Computer Science		2	1		1
	Physics		1			
	Political Science		1			
			14	1		1
189.167	**Management Trainee** ...... ESC					
	Accountancy		2	2	1	3
	Biology				1	1
	Classics				1	1

DOT	JOB TITLE	HOC	1960-1974	1975-1980 M	F	T
	Economics		2	1	1	2
	English		2			
	History		3	3		3
	Management		4	11	5	16
	Marketing		6	2		2
	Math/Computer Science		2			
	Modern Languages				1	1
	Philosophy				1	1
	Political Science		1	1		1
	Psychology				1	1
	Sociology		1			
			23	20	12	32
163.117	**Marketing Manager**	ESC				
	Accountancy		2			
	Biology		1			
	Chemistry		5			
	Economics		2			
	Education				1	1
	English		3			
	History		3	1		1
	Management		9	2		2
	Marketing		7	3	1	4
	Math/Computer Science		3			
	Natural Science		1			
	Physics		2			
	Political Science				1	1
	Sociology		2	1		1
			40	7	3	10
050.067	**Market-Research Analyst**	IAS				
	Accountancy		3			
	Chemistry		1			
	Economics		10	1		1

DOT	JOB TITLE	HOC	1960-1974	1975-1980 M	F	T
	English				1	1
	History		3			
	Management		11		1	1
	Marketing		9	4	2	6
	Math/Computer Science		5			
	Modern Languages		1			
	Political Science		1			
			44	**5**	**4**	**9**
020.067	**Mathematician**	IAS				
	Math/Computer Science		3	1	1	2
			3	**1**	**1**	**2**
070.	**Medical Doctor**	ISA				
	Accountancy		1			
	Biology		164	8	2	10
	Chemistry		14	1		1
	Classics		2			
	Economics		2			
	English		1			
	History		2			
	Management		2			
	Marketing		1			
	Natural Science		8		2	2
	Psychology		2			
	Sociology		4			
			203	**9**	**4**	**13**
— —	**Medical Student**	—				
	Accountancy			1		1
	Biology		24	40	18	58
	Chemistry		3	7	1	8
	Management			1		1

DOT	JOB TITLE	HOC	1960-1974	1975-1980 M	F	T
	Math/Computer Science		1			
	Modern Languages		1		1	1
	Natural Science		5	13	5	18
	Physics		2			
	Psychology		3		1	1
	Sociology		1			
			40	62	26	88
078.261	**Medical Technologist**	ISR				
	Biology		2	1	2	3
	Economics		1			
	Education		1			
	English		1			
	History		1			
	Natural Science		3	1	1	2
	Psychology				1	1
			9	2	4	6
025.062	**Meteorologist**	IRA				
	Political Science		1			
			1			
041.061	**Microbiologist**	IRS				
	Biology		2	1	1	2
	Chemistry		1			
			3	1	1	2
152.047	**Music Director**	ASI				
	Accountancy		1			
			1			

DOT	JOB TITLE	HOC	1960-1974	1975-1980 M	F	T
152.041	**Musician**	ASI				
	Accountancy		1			
	English		1			
	Management		1			
	Modern Languages		1			
			4			
131.267	**Newspaper Reporter**	ASI				
	Economics		1			
	English		4	1	1	2
	History		3			
	Political Science		1	1		1
	Urban Studies			1		1
			9	3	1	4
070.101	**Obstetrician**	ISA				
	(see Medical Doctor)					
169.167	**Office Manager**	ESC				
	Accountancy		21	1		1
	Biology		1			
	Chemistry		2			
	Economics		8	1		1
	English		11		1	1
	History		13			
	Management		42	7	2	9
	Marketing		12	3	1	4
	Math/Computer Science		8	1		1
	Modern Languages		2			
	Natural Science		3			
	Philosophy		1			
	Physics		3			
	Political Science		2			
	Sociology		3	1		1
	Urban Studies		3		2	2
			135	14	6	20

DOT	JOB TITLE	HOC	1960-1974	1975-1980		
				M	F	T
184.167	**Operations Manager**	ESC				
	Accountancy		8	2	1	3
	Economics		2			
	English		1			
	History		1			
	Management		7	15		15
	Marketing		5	3		3
	Math/Computer Science		4	1		1
	Natural Science		1			
	Physics		1			
	Political Science		2	1		1
	Sociology		1			
			33	22	1	23
070.101	**Ophthalmologist** .... (see Medical Doctor)	ISA				
079.101	**Optometrist**	SIR				
	Biology		1			
	Management			1		1
			1	1		1
195.167	**Parole/Probation Officer**	SIC				
	Economics		2			
	English		1			
	History		4			
	Management		2			
	Political Science		2	1		1
	Sociology		6			
			17	1		1
110.117	**Patent Attorney**	ESA				
	Chemistry		1			
			1			

DOT	JOB TITLE	HOC	1960-1974	1975-1980 M	F	T
070.101	**Pediatrician** .... (see Medical Doctor)	ISA				
166.117	**Personnel Manager**	SEC				
	Accountancy		3	1		1
	Biology		1			
	Economics		9	1		1
	Education		1			
	English		3			
	History		5	1	1	2
	Management		16	9	4	13
	Marketing		11	2	2	4
	Math/Computer Science		5			
	Modern Languages		2	1	1	2
	Political Science		3	1		1
	Psychology		1	1		1
	Sociology		5		2	2
	Urban Studies				1	1
			65	**17**	**11**	**28**
074.161	**Pharmacist**	IES				
	Biology		2			
	Economics		2			
	Natural Science		1	1		1
			5	**1**		**1**
041.061	**Pharmacologist**	IRS				
	Chemistry		1			
			1			
— —	**Pharmacy Student**	—				
	Biology		1			
			1			

DOT	JOB TITLE	HOC	1960-1974	1975-1980 M	F	T
143.062	**Photographer**	AIR				
	English		2			
	History		1			
			3			
070.101	**Physician** .... (see Medical Doctor)	ISA				
023.061	**Physicist**	IAR				
	Natural Science			1		1
	Physics		12	1		1
			12	2		2
196.263	**Pilot/Airplane**	IRC				
	English		1			
	History		1			
	Management		2			
	Marketing		1			
	Math/Computer Science			1		1
	Sociology		1			
			6	1		1
079.101	**Podiatrist**	SIR				
	Biology		3			
	Natural Science		1			
			4			
— —	**Podiatry Student**	—				
	Biology			2	1	3
				2	1	3

DOT	JOB TITLE	HOC	1960-1974	1975-1980 M	F	T
375.263	**Police Officer**	SRE				
	Accountancy		1	1		1
	Economics		4			
	Education		1			
	English			1		1
	History		5	5		5
	Management		4	7		7
	Marketing		2	1		1
	Math/Computer Science		1			
	Political Science			1		1
	Urban Studies		1	1		1
			19	17		17
189.117	**Private-Business Owner** ..	ESC				
	Accountancy		10	2		2
	Biology		2			
	Chemistry		2			
	Economics		7			
	Education		1			
	English		8		1	1
	History		12	1		1
	Management		13	1		1
	Marketing		10	2		2
	Math/Computer Science		3			
	Physics		2			
	Psychology			1		1
			70	7	1	8
163.267	**Production-Distribution Manager**	ESC				
	Biology			1		1
	English		1			
	History		2			

DOT	JOB TITLE	HOC	1960-1974	1975-1980 M	F	T
	Management		1			
	Marketing		4			
	Natural Science		1			
	Political Science		1			
			10	1		1
189.117	**Product Manager**	ESC				
	Accountancy		5	1		1
	Chemistry		4			
	Economics		3			
	English		2			
	History		3			
	Management		8	4		4
	Marketing		9	1	3	4
	Math/Computer Science		2			
	Natural Science		2			
	Political Science		1			
	Psychology			1	1	2
			39	7	4	11
183.117	**Production Manager**	ESC				
	Accountancy			1		1
	Biology		2			
	Chemistry		3			
	Economics		2	1		1
	English		1			
	History		3			
	Management		14	8	1	9
	Marketing		4	2		2
	Physics		1			
	Political Science		1			
	Sociology				1	1
	Urban Studies		1			
			32	12	2	14

DOT	JOB TITLE	HOC	1960-1974	1975-1980 M	F	T
070.107	**Psychiatrist** .... ISA (see Medical Doctor)					
070.107	**Psychoanalyst** .... ISA (see Medical Doctor)					
045.107	**Psychologist** .... SIA					
	Biology		1			
	Economics		2			
	History		4			
	Marketing			1		1
	Modern Languages		1			
	Natural Science		1		1	1
	Psychology		11	1	3	4
	Sociology		4			
	Urban Studies				1	1
			24	**2**	**5**	**7**
165.067	**Public-Relations Practitioner** .... AES					
	Economics		2			
	English		8	1	1	2
	History			1		1
	Management		5	3		3
	Marketing		4		1	1
	Math/Computer Science		1			
	Modern Languages				1	1
	Political Science		1	1		1
	Psychology		1			
	Sociology		2			
	Urban Studies				1	1
			24	**6**	**4**	**10**

DOT	JOB TITLE	HOC	1960-1974	1975-1980 M	F	T
162.157	**Purchasing Agent**	ESC				
	Accountancy		1		1	1
	Chemistry		1			
	Economics		3			
	Management		12	1	1	2
	Marketing		3	3		3
	Political Science			1		1
	Sociology		1	1		1
	Urban Studies		1	1		1
			22	**7**	**2**	**9**
012.167	**Quality-Control Engineer**	ERI				
	Chemistry		1			
	Economics		1			
	Management		1	1		1
	Marketing			1		1
	Natural Science		1	1		1
			4	**3**		**3**
070.101	**Radiologist** .... (see Medical Doctor)	ISA				
250.357	**Real-Estate Agent/ Broker**	ESC				
	Accountancy		2	1		1
	Biology		1			
	Chemistry		1			
	Economics		1			
	History				1	1
	Management		4	1	2	3
	Marketing		2	1		1
	Political Science		1	1		1
	Sociology		1			
	Urban Studies		1			
			14	**4**	**3**	**7**

DOT	JOB TITLE	HOC	1960-1974	1975-1980 M	F	T
045.107	**Rehabilitation Counselor** .... SIA					
	Biology		1			
	Economics		1			
	English		1			
	History		1			
	Management		1			
	Natural Science				1	1
	Psychology		4			
	Sociology		1			
			10		1	1
189.117	**Research-and-Development Director** .... ESC					
	Art History			1		1
	Biology		2	2	2	4
	Chemistry		6			
	Education		1			
	History		1		1	1
	Management		4		1	1
	Marketing		5			
	Math/Computer Science		2			
	Physics		2			
	Psychology		2			
	Sociology		1			
	Urban Studies		1		1	1
			27	3	5	8
160.167	**Revenue Agent** .... CES					
	Accountancy		22	3		3
	Chemistry		1			
	Classics		1			
	Economics		4			
	History				1	1
	Management		3			

DOT	JOB TITLE	HOC	1960-1974	1975-1980 M	F	T
	Marketing		1			
	Physics		1			
	Political Science		1			
			34	3	1	4
290.447	**Sales Clerk**	ESC				
	Accountancy		1	2		2
	Art History		1			
	Chemistry		1			
	Classics			1		1
	Economics		7			
	Education			1		1
	English		3			
	History		5			
	Management		14	5	1	6
	Marketing		20	6		6
	Math/Computer Science		2			
	Modern Languages		1			
	Natural Science			1		1
	Physics		1			
	Political Science		2			
	Sociology		1	1	1	1
	Urban Studies		1			
			60	17	2	18
163.167	**Sales Manager**	ESC				
	Accountancy		2	2		2
	Chemistry		2			
	Classics		2			
	Economics		8			
	Education		1			
	English		8	1	1	2

DOT	JOB TITLE	HOC	1960-1974	1975-1980 M	F	T
	History		7	1		1
	Management		24	5		5
	Marketing		27	11	1	12
	Math/Computer Science		1			
	Modern Languages		1			
	Philosophy		1			
	Political Science		1			
	Psychology		1			
	Sociology		1			
	Urban Studies		1			
			88	20	2	22
279.357	**Sales/Service Representative** .... ESC					
	Accountancy		2	2		2
	Biology		5	1	1	2
	Chemistry		6	1		1
	Economics		28	1		1
	Education		1		1	1
	English		9	2	1	3
	History		23	5		5
	Management		36	19	3	22
	Marketing		41	10	3	13
	Math/Computer Science		4			
	Modern Languages		5		3	3
	Natural Science		3	2		2
	Political Science		3	2		2
	Psychology		1			
	Sociology		8	1		1
	Urban Studies				1	1
			175	46	13	59
020.167	**Securities Analyst** .... IAS					
	Biology		1			
	Economics		5			
	Management			2		2

DOT	JOB TITLE	HOC	1960-1974	1975-1980 M	F	T
	Marketing		2			
	Political Science		1			
			9	2		2
186.167	**Securities Trader**	ESC				
	Accountancy		1			
	Economics		2	1		1
	History		3			
	Management		2	1		1
	Marketing		1			
	Sociology		1			
			10	2		2
189.167	**Security Officer**	ESC				
	Accountancy			1		1
	Economics		1			
	History		1	1		1
	Management			1		1
	Natural Science			1	1	2
	Political Science		1	1		1
	Sociology		1			
	Urban Studies		1			
			5	5	1	6
— —	**Seminarian**	—				
	History		2	1		1
	Marketing		1			
	Modern Languages		1			
	Philosophy		1			
	Political Science		1			
			6.	1		1

DOT	JOB TITLE	HOC	1960-1974	1975-1980 M	F	T
600-800	**Skilled Trades**	RIC				
	Accountancy			2	1	3
	Biology		1			
	Classics		2			
	Economics		2			
	Education		3	2		2
	English		1	1		1
	History		6	2		2
	Management		10	10		10
	Marketing		7	1		1
	Math/Computer Science		8			
	Natural Science		2			
	Philosophy		1			
	Political Science		1	1		1
	Psychology		1			
	Urban Studies		1	1		1
			46	20	1	21
188.117	**Social-Welfare Director**	ESC				
	Economics		1			
	English		1		1	1
	History		2			
	Modern Languages		3		1	1
	Political Science		1		1	
	Psychology		1			
	Sociology		1			
	Urban Studies		1		3	3
			10	1	5	6
195.107	**Social Worker**	SIC				
	Accountancy		1			
	Art History		1			
	Biology		1			

DOT	JOB TITLE	HOC	1960-1974	1975-1980 M	F	T
	Economics		2	1		1
	Education		2			
	English		7		1	1
	History		7	1		1
	Management		3	2		2
	Marketing		3		1	1
	Math/Computer Science		4			
	Modern Languages		2		2	2
	Philosophy		4			
	Political Science		6			
	Psychology		1		5	5
	Sociology		23	2	4	6
	Urban Studies		5		6	6
			72	6	19	25
054.067	**Sociologist** .... SIA					
	Management			1		1
	Sociology		1			
			1	1		1
375.167	**Special Agent/FBI** .... SRE					
	Accountancy		6	1		1
	Economics		4			
	Education		2	1		1
	History		1			
	Management		2			
	Modern Languages		1			
			16	2		2
076.107	**Speech Therapist** .... SIR					
	Psychology		1			
			1			

DOT	JOB TITLE	HOC	1960-1974	1975-1980 M	F	T
020.067	**Statistician**	IAS				
	Economics		1			
	Management		1			
	Marketing			1		1
	Math/Computer Science		1			
	Sociology				1	1
			3	**1**	**1**	**2**
251.157	**Stockbroker**	ECS				
	Accountancy		1	2		2
	Economics		2			
	English			2		2
	History		2			
	Management		2	5		5
	Marketing		5			
	Math/Computer Science		1			
	Sociology		1			
	Urban Studies			1		1
			14	**10**		**10**
185.167	**Store Manager**	ESI				
	Accountancy		1	1		1
	Classics		1			
	Economics		1			
	History		4	1		1
	Management			5		5
	Marketing		3	1	1	2
	Math/Computer Science		2	1		1
	Modern Languages		1			
	Philosophy			1		1
	Political Science		1			
	Psychology			1		1
	Sociology		1			
			15	**11**	**1**	**12**

DOT	JOB TITLE	HOC	1960-1974	1975-1980 M	F	T
070.101	**Surgeon** .... (see Medical Doctor)	ISA				
012.167	**Systems Analyst/Electronic Data Processing**	ERI				
	Accountancy		8			
	Biology		1			
	Chemistry		1			
	Classics		1			
	Economics		8	2		2
	English		4			
	History		2			
	Management		23	2		2
	Marketing		9	1		1
	Math/Computer Science		32	1		1
	Modern Languages		1			
	Natural Science		1			
	Physics		2			
	Psychology		1			
	Sociology		4			
	Urban Studies		1			
			99	6		6
003.167	**Systems Engineer**	IRE				
	Art History		1			
	Economics		2			
	History		1			
	Management		3			
	Math/Computer Science		1			
	Philosophy		1			
	Physics		3			
	Psychology		1			
			13			

DOT	JOB TITLE	HOC	1960-1974	1975-1980 M	F	T
160.162	**Tax Accountant**	CES				
	Accountancy		18	10	1	11
	Economics		1	1		1
	Education			1		1
	Marketing		1			
			20	12	1	13
160.167	**Tax Administrator**	CES				
	Accountancy		6	2		2
	Economics		1	1		1
	English		1			
	Management				1	1
			8	3	1	4
110.117	**Tax Attorney**	ESA				
	Accountancy		6			
	Economics		1			
			7			
090.227	**Teacher/College**	SIA				
	Accountancy		2			
	Art History		2			
	Biology		9	1		1
	Chemistry		8			
	Classics		5			
	Economics		7			
	Education		1		1	1
	English		24			
	History		13			
	Management		3	1		1
	Marketing		1			
	Math/Computer Science		20			
	Modern Languages		14	1		1

DOT	JOB TITLE	HOC	1960-1974	1975-1980 M	F	T
	Physics		3			
	Psychology		9			
	Sociology		10	1		1
	Urban Studies		3			
			134	4	1	5
092.227	**Teacher/Elementary School** .... SAI					
	Art History				1	1
	Biology		1	1	1	2
	Classics		3		1	1
	Economics		8	2	1	3
	Education		81	4	60	64
	English		21	2	2	4
	History		30	5	3	8
	Management		3			
	Marketing		2	1	1	2
	Math/Computer Science		5	1		1
	Modern Languages		5	1		1
	Natural Science		2		1	1
	Political Science		2	1		1
	Psychology		2		2	2
	Sociology		6		3	3
	Urban Studies		1			
			172	18	76	94
091.227	**Teacher/High School** ..... SAE					
	Accountancy		7			
	Art History		3			
	Biology		17	5	3	8
	Chemistry		5			
	Classics		7			
	Economics		14			
	Education		7	8	8	16
	English		86	2	3	5

DOT	JOB TITLE	HOC	1960-1974	1975-1980 M	F	T
	History		72	7	2	9
	Management		17	2	3	5
	Marketing		17	1		1
	Math/Computer Science		61	4	6	10
	Modern Languages		34		1	1
	Natural Science		10	3	2	5
	Philosophy		3			
	Physics		7	1		1
	Political Science		10			
	Psychology		2	1	2	3
	Sociology		10	3	1	4
	Urban Studies		1			
			390	**37**	**31**	**68**
099.227	**Teacher/Other**	SIR				
	Accountancy		1	1		1
	Biology		3	1		1
	Chemistry		2	1		1
	Classics		1			
	Economics		2			
	Education		15	1	21	22
	English		16	1	4	5
	History		21	1		1
	Management		4	1	2	3
	Marketing		4		1	1
	Math/Computer Science		13		2	2
	Modern Languages		10	1	1	2
	Natural Science		2		1	1
	Physics		1			
	Political Science		2			
	Psychology		2	2		2
	Sociology		9		1	1
	Urban Studies		1	1	1	2
			109	**11**	**34**	**45**

DOT	JOB TITLE	HOC	1960-1974	1975-1980 M	F	T
094.227	**Teacher/Special Education** .... SAI					
	Education		1	2	4	6
	English		1			
	History		1			
	Marketing			1		1
	Math/Computer Science		1			
	Modern Languages		1			
	Psychology			1		1
			5	4	4	8
159.147	**Television/Radio Personnel** .... AES					
	Accountancy			1		1
	Economics		1			
	English		1			
	Modern Languages		1			
	Psychology			1		1
	Sociology		1			
			4	2		2
184.117	**Traffic Analyst/ Manager** .... ESC					
	Accountancy		1	1		1
	Art History				1	1
	Economics		2	1		1
	English		1		1	1
	History		2	1		1
	Management		5	3		3
	Marketing		1	2	1	3
			12	8	3	11
166.227	**Training Specialist** .... SEC					
	Economics		1			
	Education				1	1
	English		2			

DOT	JOB TITLE	HOC	1960-1974	1975-1980 M	F	T
	History		5			
	Management			1		1
	Marketing		1			
	Math/Computer Science		1			
	Political Science		1			
	Sociology		1			
			12	1	1	2
137.267	**Translator**	ASI				
	Management		1			
	Modern Languages		1		1	1
			2		1	1
184.117	**Transportation Manager** ..	ESC				
	Biology				1	1
	Economics		1			
	History		1	1		1
	Management		4	2		2
	Marketing		1	1		1
	Natural Science			1		1
	Sociology			1		1
	Urban Studies			1		1
			7	7	1	8
252.157	**Travel Agent**	ECS				
	Education		1		2	2
	English		1			
			2		2	2
186.117	**Trust Officer/Bank**	ESC				
	Accountancy			1		1
	Economics		7			
	Management		4			

DOT	JOB TITLE	HOC	1960-1974	1975-1980 M	F	T
	Marketing		1		1	1
	Math/Computer Science		1			
	Political Science		1			
			14	**1**	**1**	**2**
199.167	**Urban Planner**	ICR				
	Economics		2			
	History		1			
	Marketing		1			
	Natural Science				1	1
	Political Science		2			
	Sociology		4		1	1
	Urban Studies		1	1		1
			11	**1**	**2**	**3**
070.101	**Urologist** .... (see Medical Doctor)	ISA				
073.101	**Veterinarian**	IRS				
	Accountancy		1			
	Biology		1		1	1
	Natural Science		1			
			3		**1**	**1**
045.107	**Vocational Counselor**	SIA				
	English		1			
	Political Science			1		1
	Psychology		2	1	1	2
	Sociology		1			
	Urban Studies		3		1	1
			7	**2**	**2**	**4**

DOT	JOB TITLE	HOC	1960-1974	1975-1980		
				M	F	T
131.067	**Writer/Fiction and Nonfiction**	ASI				
	English		2			
	Political Science		1			
	Sociology		1			
			4			
131.267	**Writer/Technical**	ASI				
	Economics		1			
	English		3	2		2
	Marketing		1			
			5	2		2

ABOUT THE AUTHORS

Lawrence R. Malnig earned his B.A. in French at Brooklyn College, his M.A. in Italian and Spanish at Columbia University, and his Ph.D. in Counseling Psychology at New York University. In 1951, he founded the Counseling Center at Saint Peter's College and since that time has had an abiding interest in the psychological needs of students, and in the outcomes of their education. With L. Augustine Grady, S.J., and Dr. Thaddeus V. Tuleja, he published the first survey of the Saint Peter's College alumni titled *Peacocks On Parade* which won national recognition. His more than 25 articles in newspapers, and in popular and professional magazines, include *Anxiety and Academic Prediction; Uptight Students;* and *Teen-Ager: Rebel With A Cause.* He has served on the editorial boards of The Catholic Psychological Record and The Vocational Guidance Quarterly. In addition to campus counseling and career-options research, Dr. Malnig conducts a private practice in psychotherapy and is Psychological Consultant in Communication and Administration to diploma and collegiate nursing schools. In his Ridgefield, New Jersey, community, he has served on the Board of Education and The Mayor's Environmental Committee. He is a member of the Board of Trustees of Elizabeth Seton College in Westchester County, New York.

Anita Malnig, a 1971 graduate, is herself a statistic in this book. After majoring in English Literature, she began her writing and editing career at the Golden Book Division of Western Publishing Company. She edited *Children's Playcraft* and *Children's Digest* for Parents Magazine Enterprises and served as children's book editor for Random House and Children's Television Workshop. She has published five of her own books and taught a course in book publishing in the New York University Continuing Education Program. Ms. Malnig, a consulting editor for a children's computer magazine, is also writing a series of nature books. She lives and works in San Francisco.

A special word of thanks to James C.G. Conniff, whose expertise did much to make this book the useful instrument we want it to be.

DATE DUE

DEC. 0 2 1991	DEC 2 '91		
AUG. 29 1993			

HIGHSMITH 45-220